Malaysia's National Language Policy

Malaysia's National Language Policy and the Legal System

Richard Mead

Monograph Series 30/Yale University Southeast Asia Studies
Yale Center for International and Area Studies

Library of Congress Catalog Card Number: 87-050360
International Standard Book Number: 0-938692-30-5

New Haven, Connecticut 06520

Distributor:
Yale University Southeast Asia Studies
Box 13A Yale Station
New Haven, Connecticut 06520

Printed in the U.S.A.

For my mother and in memory of my father.

Contents

THE AUTHOR

Richard Mead is a sociolinguist teaching at the J.L. Kellogg Graduate School of Management, Northwestern University, and the Graduate Institute of Business Administration, Thailand. In 1980-83, he worked in Universiti Malaya, Malaysia, in Legal English Syllabuses. He is currently interested in cross-cultural management in a South-East Asian context.

Acknowledgements

This monograph grew out of research undertaken at the Universiti Malaya from 1980 to 1983. I benefited greatly from discussions with political scientists, sociolinguists, legal practitioners, and scholars in Malaysia, the United Kingdom, and the United States. In particular, I have to thank Dr. Ruth McVey, then of the School of Oriental and African Studies, and Professor Dan Lev of the University of Washington. I owe most to my wife, Kullada Kesboonchoo of Chulalongkorn University, Thailand, who spent considerable time reading through the earlier drafts and made many invaluable suggestions. The final draft was prepared at the Graduate Institute of Business Administration, Chulalongkorn University, and I am very grateful to the Director, Professor Toemsakdi Krishnamra, for his support and encouragement. It was type by Jongjit Wongverawattanagul and Vimol Pruekwatthanachai.

I must emphasize that the conclusions reached in this monograph are strictly my own and should not be thought to represent the opinions of any of those persons listed above.

CHAPTER ONE

The Break With The Past

Introduction

In early October, the Chief Registrar to the Courts of Malaysia issued a Directive requiring that from the fifth of that month

- all letters on matters of legal administration should be written in Malay.
- evidence given by witnesses should be directly translated into Malay.
- arguments by lawyers should be given in Malay.
- presidents of Sessions Courts and magistrates should write down their judgements in Malay.
- speeches made in legal ceremonies should be in Malay.[1]

These requirements were subject to the provision that the use of Malay should not injure the cause of justice.[2]

This monograph deals with the significance of that Directive. At times the argument seems to stray a considerable distance—to education policy and enrollments in national universities, to ambitions of political parties, and to the provisions of the national cultural policy. But each apparent digression leads back to the same points of contention: why was the Directive thought necessary? What was it intended to achieve? Who supported it and who opposed it?

For several months before the Directive was issued, vague and contradictory rumors circulated that at last a decision had been made to impose the use of Malay in the legal system. In February 1981, staff of the Attorney-General's Chambers were required to write legal opinions and correspondence in Malay.[3] In June, a Deputy Minister in the Prime Minister's Department announced that all cases in lower courts would be conducted in Malay "soon," but only when "all relevant law books and documents had been translated."[4] He explained that "he could not say exactly when the move would be implemented,"[5] but it might be by the end of the year, and use of Malay would be compulsory.[6] On 25 September it was reported that "the Government has decided to introduce Bahasa Malaysia in the lower courts in 1983."[7] But only one week later the Directive was issued.

The Directive did not constitute an isolated event, but represented one stage in a drawn-out campaign to assert Malay as the national and official language. Since the 1920s, supposedly cultural and literary societies had fostered the use of

Malay as a means of expressing Malay nationalism (Mohamed Aris Haji Othman 1980). The national language policy had been officially sanctioned by the Independence Constitution of 1957, and successfully implemented in the education system. But still the law of the land was practised in English. Two questions are pursued throughout this monograph:

Why was language policy not implemented in the legal system before 1981?

Why was language policy implemented then?

The monograph argues that the Directive signified more than an attempt to remove the anomolous status of English in the courts and to fully implement the use of Malay. The delay and then the decision to go ahead were determined by conflicting notions of the role of law in society, and by evolving political, social, and cultural priorities. We are obliged to take account of a range of influences, and each box opened reveals a further box. This introductory section focusses on the relevance of language planning to Malaysian society, and the plan to replace English as the language of the law. The second section, *The Political Setting*, sketches in the political and cultural contexts, and looks at some of the features that influenced the decision to implement policy.

A note on the methodology applied in this monograph is appropriate here. A distinction is made between primary data, to be explained, and the context. The selection of primary data is rule-governed. They are culled from the period between late 1980 and early 1983. These months saw a change of administration and a quickening of the pace of change in Malaysian society. The data come from the English-language press and transcriptions of courtroom proceedings. The history of the years preceding 1980 is treated very much as the sociolinguist treats his categories of linguistic and situational context, as distinct from the fragment under analysis, and as predictive influences of which the datum represents a summation. This relationship is illustrated by an invented interaction. The reader is invited to puzzle out where Speaker A and Speaker B are situated, what is happening, and what information each utterance is intended to convey.

Speaker A: Telephone.
Speaker B: I'm in the bath.
Speaker A: Okay.

The datum is itself predictive, and we infer that Speaker A will answer the telephone. But precisely how he formulates his response to the caller lies outside the formal scope of the enquiry. Similarly, this study does not attempt to bring history up to date, and is limited to the predictive relationship between context from which the primary data derive and the primary data. So we focus on the events of approximately thirty months, and do not attempt to justify this analysis in terms of what happened next.

The formulation of language policy and its implementation is first of all a matter of language planning. Language planning in a developing nation implies specifying a goal of language usage, then mapping out the routes by which that goal should be achieved. Functions of usage are designated, new usages prescribed, and actual usages rationalized. Grammar and vocabulary are standardized. Language planning serves the instrumental functions of interpreting the technologies and cultures of the outside world into a local frame of reference, and of fashioning a medium for centralizing political control. In Malaysia, as in other ethnically divided developing countries, language planning created a tool both for integrating the state on the basis of the politically dominant ethnic group, and for creating a symbol of national unity and identity.

Two points may be inferred. Governments endorse language planning only as a means for achieving some other political, social, and economic end. Language planning does not constitute an end in itself. Electorates do not need to be convinced of the value of a better health service or cheaper food, but they do expect to be told the advantages of no longer using language A to perform function Z and using language B instead. The Malaysian experience during the months under review demonstrates how language planning is constrained by the political and social context, and how it affects this context. Second, the importance invested in language planning varies according to the homogeneity of the culture and the language. In neighbouring Thailand, for instance, regional variations are comparatively slight and ethnic minorities relatively assimilated. The initial drive to nationalism in the late nineteenth and early twentieth centuries concentrated on establishing centralised political, bureaucratic, and economic structures. Kullada Kesboonchoo (1984) shows that King Chulalongkorn's education reforms were directed to these ends, and paid far less attention to imposing Central Thai language and culture on the peripheries. But the Malaysian experience is a very different kettle of fish.

The communal, demographic, cultural, and economic fissures that beset the country militated against the natural evolution of a sense of unity and common identity. The population of 14.5 million was appropriately 51 per cent Malay, 38 per cent Chinese, and 11 per cent Indian. The Malays followed Islam and despite the fact that they accounted for most of the recent urban growth—up from 2.5 million in 1970 to about 4.1 million in 1980 (Fisk 1982, p. 10)—approximately 85 per cent lived in rural areas and followed rural occupations (Husin Ali 1981, pp. 80-84). In 1973 their mean household income amounted to US$242 (figures quoted in M. Zainudin Salleh and Zulkifly Osman 1982, p. 143). The Chinese were Confucian, Buddhist, Taoist, or Christian (Catholic or Protestant), with a mean household income of US$534. They were mainly urban and, like their fellow immigrants the Indians, specialised in the modern sector of the economy—commerce, services, mining, and large-scale commercial agriculture. The Indians were Hindu, Sikh, Muslim, or Christian (Catholic or Protestant), with a mean household income of US$408.

In this extreme example of a multi-ethnic society, language had a peculiar significance for political and social development, and language planning assumed great importance. The colonial language English still enjoyed prestige but was spoken at all fluently by less than ten per cent of the population. Few Malaysians other than the Malays spoke Malay as a mother tongue. The Chinese and Indians accepted the status of Malay as the official language, but argued that its area of official application should be severely restricted. Their own mother tongues symbolized their communal identities: among the Chinese, Hokkien (34.2 per cent), Hakka (22.1 per cent), Cantonese (19.8 per cent), Teochew (12.4 per cent), Hainanese (4.7 per cent), Kwongsai (2.5 per cent), Hockchiu (1.8 per cent), Henghua (0.5 per cent), Hockchia (0.3 per cent), others (1.7 per cent); among the Indians, Tamil (80.9 per cent), Malayali, Punjabi, Telugu, Urdu, Gujerati, Singhalese, etc.; among the "official" Malays of Sarawak, Iban, and of Sabah, Kadazan. These official 1970 figures, which do not distinguish Mandarin, are quoted in Asmah Haji Omar 1979, where the discussion of Malaysian language planning gives a planner's point of view (reviewed in Mead 1983). In this situation, some centralized language planning was needed if a common national identity were to be generated and non-Malays were to be persuaded that it was in their interests to give priority to speaking and writing in Malay. The realisation of this ideal still lies in the future. Chinese may talk to Malays in Malay, but seldom to other Chinese. One informant told me, "If two Chinese don't share a common (Chinese) language, then they use English. But if they don't speak English either, they don't bother. If one of them started to use Malay, he would lose face."

English, then, might still function as a *lingua franca* in informal settings. And until 1981, it carried the same function in the highly formal setting of the law court. There were historical reasons for this.

The colonists had introduced English common law to the Malay settlements (albeit modified to local circumstances: Bartholomew 1976)[8] at the onset of their competition. Independent Malaysia still employed the system and shared this characteristic with many other ex-colonies whose legal institutions had not been affected by Independence (Athuluthmudal 1962, p. 223). However, the application of English law was subject to two limitations.

> Firstly, it is applied only in the absence of local statutes on the particular subjects. Local law takes precedence over English law as the latter is meant only to fill in gaps in the local system. Secondly, only that part of the English law that is suited to local circumstances will be applied. The proviso to section 3(1) of the Civil Law Act is the authority for this. (Wu Min Aun 1975, p. 20).

But in practice these limitations appeared to be highly restricted and in 1983 at least ninety per cent of Malaysia's laws were calculated to come from England.[9]

Not only were Malaysia's laws borrowed from England but they were implemented within an essentially English legal system. Local legislation was introduced into Parliament by a Private Bill, Private Member's Bill, Hybrid Bill, or Government Bill. After passing through the debate and committee stages of the House in which it originated, it was sent on to the other House. If approved by both Houses, it was sent on to the *Yang di-Pertuan Agong* (King) for the Royal assent. The King had powers to delay enactment but not to vote. He also acted as the highest local court of appeal. Below him sat the Federal Court, then the High Courts, the Sessions Courts, the Magistrates' Courts, and lastly the *Penghulu* (Headman's) Courts. We are only very marginally concerned here with *Penghulu* Courts, which implement customary law based on *adat* (the basic land tenure system; see Hooker 1972) in an extremely limited and local jurisdiction, and with the Muslim Shariah Courts, which enforced religious observances and regulated the matrimonial lives of Muslims and had no direct link with the civil court system. Appeals from the Muslim Courts were heard by Special Appeal Boards, not by the High Court or Federal Court (Ahmad Ibrahim 1976).

The principle of precedent applied. The Federal Court decided appeals and its decisions bound itself and all lower courts. A High Court decision bound subordinate courts, but one High Court judge was not bound to follow the decision made by another. The decisions of Sessions and Magistrates' Courts were not binding on any court. (For a further discussion of the Malaysian legal system, see Wu Min Aun's excellent introduction to the subject, 1975).

There were differences between the Malaysian and English systems; for instance, the jury system had very restricted application. But by and large, an English barrister licensed to practise in Malaysian courts was immediately at home. In Malaysia before the Directive was issued, unlike in many other ex-colonial jurisdictions, he could be almost certain of finding the case conducted in his native tongue. This continued use of an English system practised in the medium of English was politically significant.

It is useful to distinguish here between the promulgation of a legal system and its implementation in the courts. In any nation the law both creates and expresses political and social control, and constitutes an arm of state power. Officers of the court make decisions that interpret the laws and coerce obedience to the state. They can call upon the police and, if necessary, the armed forces in order to support these decisions. The individual influences the promulgation of laws only to the extent that he influences the political process. The content of laws and the organization of the legal system reflect the interests of the political power holders. This is particularly evident in the wake of a successful revolution. The 1787 American Constitution maximized the freedom of property-holding individuals who had contributed most energetically to the revolutionary cause, and decentralized the power of governmental institutions in an attempt to minimize the likelihood of a new tyranny. Similarly, the principles expressed in the 1917 Soviet Constitution reflected Marxist-Leninist ideals of the relationship between the state and the proletariat.

Britain applied English common law to its overseas possessions because of the advantages in enforcing a system that applied colonial values and was accessible to the colonial authorities. It might be argued that in 1957, independent Malaya was forced to continue employing the English system because the country lacked an indigenous system above the level of the Penghulu Courts. But this does not explain why the system should have been continued for so long after Independence and in the medium of English. The evidence suggests that the leaders of Malaya (Malaysia in 1963) perceived it to be working in their own best interests.

At the level of implementation, the law is correctly administered only when the prescribed procedures are followed, in an appropriate place, and by qualified initiates. In the courtroom, the layman who does not know the rules is very much at the mercy of the professional who does.

Procedural rules are enforced in ritualised behavior and most particularly by language. Danet (1980, p. 448) draws attention to the "interrelations" between language and law.

> Words are obviously of paramount importance in the law; in a most basic sense, the law would not exist without language. Compare the roles of language in medicine and law: to practice medicine is primarily (though not exclusively) to work with physical substances, to relate to human bodies as physical objects. To practice law, on the other hand, is to relate to people as social beings, as "language animals" (Steiner 1968; Winch 1958).

Danet writes within the traditions of legal anthropology set by Malinowski (1934), and deals with the functions of law rather than its forms, and the functions of language when employed in the "negotiation of social order" (Danet, p. 449). In showing how Malaysian courtroom procedure influenced implemenation of the language policy, chapter four emphasizes the same point.

The Chief Registrar's Directive that all letters should be written in Malay, all evidence translated into Malay, all arguments given in Malay, all judgments written in Malay, and all speeches made in Malay attempted to control by promulgating a regulation. The subsequent condition, that the use of Malay should not injure the cause of justice, indicated the possibilities for compromise. "Justice" here seems to mean that the system should be administered fairly, and fairly within the eyes of society. That is, implementation of the Directive should take account of communal and political realities.

Hence the authors of the Directive attempted to impose conformity on the courts but they also recognised the need to retain public sympathy with the legal system's application to individual cases. This might seem commonplace. But this problem of establishing legal legitimacy should be given due consideration. The extreme heterogeneity of Malaysian society has been noted, and the authorities were necessarily sensitive to the practical problems of imposing their mandate on the different communities. As we shall see, the political debate of "sensitive issues" was discouraged. Second, Malay, not English, was the official language, and yet twenty-four years after Independence the Government found it necessary to impose Malay as the medium of the law in place of English which was spoken as a first language by a very small percentage of the population, and at all fluently by only about ten per cent. Thus it is necessary to explain why the legal system enjoyed legitimacy as a social institution while it was practised for so long in a foreign language. Notions of legal legitimacy are tackled generally in the literature devoted to legal philosophy (see Hart 1961 for a seminal work, and Dworkin 1977 and Morawetz 1980 for more recent discussion of the issues raised). The problem has been redefined here in political terms. Hence the questions raised at the beginning of this section: why was the switch to Malay not made before 1981? Why was it made then? We now go on to examine the political context and the ideology that the Directive expressed.

The Political Setting

The two questions posed above can be taken to imply that the Directive constituted a radical change of direction. This is simply demonstrated if we limit our answer to the legal system. It had hitherto been relatively unscathed by language policy. However, an interpretation of the Directive that is restricted to judicial issues and that does not explain how political and cultural factors constrained implementation and were affected by it is inadequately narrow. By some criteria, the significant shifts in policy had been made well before 1981, and the Directive was merely symptomatic.

Insofar as the Directive represented one more stage in a continuous process of implementing the use of the national language and forging national unity, the reform of the courts was a logical development of policies decided before Independence. These policies were designed to overcome the horrendous social, economic, and cultural cleavages that were noted in the introductory section. Insofar as the Directive signalled a new departure, it signalled that the language policies of 1957 were no longer effective in a new world. A case can be made for both points of view. This section demonstrates how a number of significant events in the development of modern Malaysia can be read as continuing or breaking away from tradition. These contextualize the discussion that follows in subsequent chapters.

Early in the twentieth century, colonial Malaya consisted of three types of administration: the Straits Settlements of Malacca, Penang, and Singapore, and the Federated and Unfederated Malay States, in which the powers of the traditional rulers were heavily qualified by their British residents and advisers. This disparate system of control was remarkably stable at a time when nationalist movements elsewhere were gathering force. Then, and for a long time after, political activity was communal rather than nationalistic. Each of the three communities devoted its energies to protecting its own economic and cultural interests, and saw little benefit in building cross-communal ties (Lee Kam Hing 1981). The British had introduced the immigrant communities of Chinese and Indians originally in order to perform specific economic roles, and they were interested in perpetuating these divisions. The elites of the communities were alike in that they supported the status quo. The masses stood behind their elites (albeit in very different relationships), and any attempts to mobilize anti-British feeling on a cross-communal basis failed dismally. This phenomenon of common interest in protecting communal distinctions is a recurring theme in the development of modern Malaysia.

Post-war British policy centred on giving up political (if not economic) responsibilities wherever feasible, and Malaya was offered the alternative of a staged program leading to at least some measure of self-government. The old colonial policy of maintaining communal divisions could only retard the development of an independent nation, and the program was conditional on an agreed sharing of power among the communities. The Malayan Union Plan (1946) attempted to bring together into a unitary state all states and settlements with the exception of Singapore. Malay unhappiness was intense over the liberalized citizenship requirements that promised to benefit the non-Malays, and the restrictions on the traditional rulers' power. The United Malay National Organization (UMNO) was formed that year to lead the opposition. The subsequent renegotiation of the Union Plan and the establishment of the Federation of Malaya (1948) rebounded to the young party's credit, and won for it the commanding position in Malay and national politics that it has never surrendered. The opposition to British policies during the two years of the Union never approached violence. Relations between the British and Malay elites continued to be civil, and the Federation was celebrated as a new accord between the colonial authorities and UMNO.

The Chinese elites had their own reasons for wishing to work closely with their British and Malay counterparts. In their search for a formula by which some responsibility for government might be divested to the Malayans, the British had fostered moderate leaders in all three communities. Winning popular Chinese support for the campaign against the Malayan Communist Party (MCP) now became a priority. The MCP was led by members of the Chinese-educated intelligentsia, and the administration turned to the western-educated businessmen who made up the Chinese elite (Heng Pek Koon 1980). These leaders feared the spread of communism among their masses, and reciprocated the support given to the foundation of the Malayan (Malaysian in 1963) Chinese Association (MCA) in 1949. They wanted a permanent and national role for their community, and employed their social and personal ties with the similarly westernized Malay elite to build bridges with the UMNO leadership.

Relations between the elites and the political parties that they usually seemed able to shape in their own images were illustrated by the events of the

1951 Kuala Lumpur municipal elections. To his apparent surprise, Dato Onn bin Jaafar, the first leader of UMNO, had failed to persuade the party that it should shed its communalism and open the membership to all races. He had gone on to found the multi-racial Independence of Malaya Party (IMP). UMNO and the MCA were each dedicated primarily to the interests of their communities and to cooperation where possible and necessary with the other communities. In other words, communal interests were to be subordinated where they conflicted with the new Government's interpretation of national purpose.

The 1951 electorate demonstrated how greatly it feared to cross the communal barricades; the IMP took only two seats and the UMNO-MCA alliance won the other twelve. The IMP soon disappeared. The leaders of UMNO and the MCA recognised that the British would not hand over power to UMNO alone; the alliance became institutionalised and in 1951 was joined by the Malayan (Malaysian in 1963) Indian Congress (MIC).

The UMNO leaders enjoyed the political legitimacy that their community traditionally accorded to members of royal households. The non-Malay elites derived their status from their wealth, business connections, and in particular their cultural and personal connections with their UMNO colleagues (Wang Gungwu 1981, pp. 232-48). The MCA leaders could demonstrate that when they gave advice, UMNO listened—a role to which the Chinese-educated intelligentsia could not aspire. But their hold on their rank and file was always weaker. They had the task of justifying to UMNO their political worth as Alliance members, and at the same time convincing their memberships that compromise was often to the advantage of the non-Malays and should not be equated with surrender.

The Alliance leaders held their communities in line in the run up to Independence. The Constitution, proposed by the Reid Commission, was accepted with very little dissent. The new nation thus acquired a constitutional monarchy, a parliamentary bicameral legislature which centred power in the lower house, an executive patterned on the colonial and British model, a prime ministerial and cabinet system, regular elections, an independent judiciary that allowed for final appeals to the Privy Council in London; in other words, a constitution that closely resembled the Westminister model. Even those articles that made allowance for the local context continued policies formulated by the colonial administration. For instance, the federal organization protected the established rights of the rulers and Article 153 endorsed the "special position of the Malays and the legitimate interests of other communities" (Milne and Mauzy 1980, p. 39). According to Lee Kam Hing (1981),

> the constitution represented compromise and reflected the outlook of the political elite who accepted Western political institutions as instruments of change. (p. 247)

The question of how these institutions could fashion change in a non-Western society was still open.

The early years, then, provided a wealth of evidence to illustrate the theme of administrative continuity. The new government did not introduce any radical reforms in the machinery of state that it had inherited from the colonial power, and Independence amounted to little more than a constitutional hiccup. The abiding problem of communal differences had its roots in early pre-colonial policy, and attempts to solve it also predated Independence. The formula of communal parties cooperating in Government at the highest level continued to find electoral favour, and alternatives offered by non-Alliance parties failed. The IMP, the People's Action Party (PAP) of Singapore, the strongly Islamic Pan-Malayan Islamic Party (PMIP)—later reorganised as *Parti Islam* (PAS), the initially multi-communal and then progressively Chinese-dominated Democratic Action Party (DAP), Gerakan, the MCP, and other parties all offered alternatives to the Alliance formula at one time or another. The UMNO-dominated Alliance held them all off and has held power continuously.

The 1969 communal riots severely shook the structure of communal compromise. The elections held a few days before had focussed attention on the communal issues of the economic imbalance and the national language. Although an Alliance administration was returned, the prestige enjoyed by the consensus-minded Prime Minister, Tunku Abdul Rahman, was badly damaged. The MCA had failed to turn out the Chinese vote in the numbers expected, and even many Malays had withheld their support from the ticket. The riots gave extra-parliamentary expression to frustrations which arose from non-Malay impatience with the Malay control of access to political power, Malay fears that they were losing power within their own house, and frustrations that the guarantees given of Malay language rights, particularly in education, had not been met. They gave notice that the communal contract (Von Vorys 1976) had failed to satisfy either side, and that the Government should take Malay demands seriously. This meant adopting a considerably tougher and less accommodating attitude to non-Malay aspirations.

The legislation in the years that followed the riots was instrumental in revising the relationship between the communities. In the next chapter we shall look at the Sedition Act, the new emphasis on Malay culture, and the new edge given to implementation in the National Language Act. The Alliance was reborn in the form of the *Barisan Nasional* or National Front (1974), to which a number of smaller parties were admitted. The old practice of elite accommodation was followed, but UMNO enforced its dominance more strongly than before (Mauzy 1983, pp. 139-41). Efforts were now concentrated on anticipating and heading off communal conflicts rather than merely responding to them as they occurred (Esman 1972 pp. 258-61). The New Economic Policy (NEP) demonstrated the new bite given to pro-Malay policies. It was designed to increase national income by developing new sectors of the economy and lessening the extent of foreign control, and then to redistribute the gains. No one should lose, but the poor, and in particular the poor Malays, were intended to benefit disproportionately. In practice it restrained non-Malay expansion and worked very much to the advantage of the Malays. Employment and investment targets were set; all companies above a certain size were obliged to employ a quota of at least 30 per cent Malays at all levels, and the infrastructure was expanded and the modern sector developed with an eye to Malays owning and managing at least 30 per cent of all industrial and commercial organisations within twenty years. New educational and training facilities were created. The NEP was instrumental in the rapid growth of the Malay middle class and even a Malay capitalist class. How far the kampong Malay benefited continued to be a source of contention (Zakaria Haji Ahmad 1982, p. 89).

The new direction also had the important affect of bringing back to favour those so-called "ultras" in UMNO who had been most critical of the Tunku's laissez-faire approach to the nation's problems and had advocated a stronger pro-Malay line (Funston 1980, pp. 240-41). Their number included Dr. Mahathir bin Mohamed, whose personal attack on the Tunku after the 1969 riots had been punished by temporary expulsion from the party.

The first three Prime Ministers, Tunku Abdul Rahman, Tun Abdul Razak, and Datuk Hussein Onn all enjoyed royal connections. They had studied in English and their culture was in many respects English. All had trained as lawyers within the English system. These factors may explain the reluctance of their administrations to jettison the institutions of British political culture and, in particular, a legal system that was essentially English and practised in the medium of English.

The Tunku's two successors enjoyed the loyalty usually accorded by Malays to their political leaders—at least in public (Chandra Muzaffar 1979, ch. 5). Despite the worries that continued to shake UMNO after 1969, they succeeded in rising above party divisions. Despite their connections with the old policies, they recognised the need to defuse Malay discontent. Hence they gave the "ultras" their discrete support. In 1974 Tun Abdul Razak appointed the rehabilitated Dr. Mahathir to the cabinet, and on the Tun's death in 1976, Datuk Hussein Onn made him Deputy Prime Minister. So Dr. Mahathir's accession to power was in no way a coup. The custom that the Deputy stepped into the departing Prime Minister's shoes had been observed.

Nevertheless the new administration was of novel character, and this is illustrated by the decision to issue the Directive and to implement the language policy in the courts. Neither the Prime Minister, nor his deputy, Datuk Musa Hitam, belonged to that English-educated generation of Malay leaders that had negotiated Independence with the colonial power and then gone on to agree on the political and economic divisions with the non-Malay leaders. They were not tarred by those policies that had led to the conflagration of 1969. Dr. Mahathir had trained not as a lawyer but as a doctor. He lacked the royal connections of his predecessors and could not appeal to the kampong Malays' respect for royal authority. But his advocacy of Malay rights had won him a constituency among those Malays dissatisfied with previous policies, and in particular the emerging Malay middle class. Furthermore he adopted policies that sustained and built on this support.

Class analysis provides the Malaysian scholar with one more useful tool, but a tool to be employed with discretion. In the early eighties only two groups showed much sign of class consciousness. First were the royal families to which Dr. Mahathir's predecessors had belonged. They had acquiesced in the British exercise of colonial power and in the terms under which Independence was negotiated. Their class was

> usually more modern, more tolerant, and less tradition-bound than the sub-elites in Malay society, represented by the Malay teachers in the kampong schools, the religious teachers, and the Islamic clergy. The explanation can be found in the education which the Malay aristocracy received, nearly always in English schools, often followed by study abroad. (Means 1970, 1976, pp. 194-95).

These were admirable qualities, perhaps, but they strongly reflected the colonial past, and past values seemed increasingly removed from present day realities. To take an example, one member of a royal family told me she had spoken English at home with her father and bazaar Malay with her mother, then studied in England at secondary school and university up to a second degree. On her return to Malaysia, she found her Malay not up to examination standard, and without the all-important language qualification she was unable to find employment in the civil service or a nationalised industry.

The years after 1969 illustrated discontinuity insofar as the power of the royal families and their political allies was beginning to wane and that of the new Malay middle class to wax. The Malay middle class owed its growth to the new pro-Malay policies and the accent on modernization and the development of an urban industrialized economy. They may have been only one generation removed from the kampongs, but their loyalties to the feudal institutions of rural life had been weakened. They energetically entered the old game of collecting royal titles; according to Chandra Muzaffar (1979), over 112,000 titles and honours were awarded at the Federal level between 1958 and 1979 (p. 109). But this reflected the social rather than political importance of the royalty. The new Malay middle class had learnt the lessons of 1969. Political power had little value unless based on economic power, and the levers of economic power had to be wrested from both the foreign investor and from the Chinese businessman. (To take one 1970 example, in the corporate sector of modern agriculture, Malays owned only 0.3 per cent of the acreage, the Chinese owned 26 per cent, and foreigners owned

70.8 per cent; discussed in Higgins 1982.) They demanded Malaysian nationalism abroad and Malay nationalism at home. They would live with the immigrant races on their own terms, and not on the terms set by the Reid Commission and by old-school politicians identified with the compromise reached with the British.

The interests of the new Malay middle class did mirror those of the older class at one point. If they were to spearhead Malay economic development and compete with the Chinese, they needed an international language. They needed to be bilingual in Malay and English. So paradoxically, those children of the kampong who had provided the support for the first Prime Minister educated in Malay, competed to send their own children to the same universities in the English-speaking world that had instructed traditional rulers.[10] But an important difference lay in the values associated with this education. Now it was desired for its utilitarian benefits rather than for the cultural and social ties it offered with the cream of the British elite. British universities discovered that the cabala, "a British education" no longer performed its old magic, and that if they wished to attract Malaysian students, they were obliged to offer their wares alongside their American, Australian, and Canadian competitors, and to disseminate brochures, recruiting officers, and introductory seminars. The new class looked for some guarantee of a relevant material return on their educational investments.

Dr. Mahathir proclaimed the national coming of age in terms designed to appeal to the Malays' economic and cultural needs. His administration nursed a suspicion of the Commonwealth which seemed to offer out-of-date ideals and little that was concrete to a developing nation. The "Look East" policy of learning from the economic performances of Japan and, to a lesser extent Korea, and of encouraging investment from these countries was hedged with promises that the introduction of Japanese work ethics should not be interpreted as acceptance of Japanese cultural values.[11] In other words, emergent Malay political and cultural power would not be compromised by economic considerations. On the contrary, an aggressive economic policy provided one means of advancing Malay and Malaysian interests. A number of attempts were made to take over British companies dealing in commodities—in the cases of Guthrie Corporation, Barlow Estates, and Dunlop Estates, successfully (although ultimate control over commodity prices still appeared to reside in the London Commodity Market; see Hua Wu Yin 1983, pp. 185-86). This economic war of independence broke no more new ground than did the implementation of the language policy in the legal system; between 1971 and 1980 the foreign share of assets had fallen from 62 per cent to 48 per cent,[12] and Dr. Mahathir was merely continuing an established policy. But it was voiced with an aggression and a sense of injured pride that had not previously characterised relationships with the West, and in particular with the United Kingdom. The message was designed for a new audience.

The middle classes of all communities had more and more in common,[13] and were increasingly distanced from the poorer members of their communities. Fisk (1982) suggests that

> the conditions are now emerging in which the polarization between rich and poor could begin to transcend racial barriers. (p. 9).

This presupposes that the masses of each community developed a new consciousness of their common interests. Cham (1975) correctly insists that the lower classes constituted the vast majority, and that the Malay fisherman and Chinese rubber tapper have a common interest. However, the support that they continued to give their communal parties suggests that notions of communal identity still overruled any consciousness of common class. It might be that the nation's ills arose from the Alliance elite exploiting and exacerbating language, cultural, and religious differences in order to maintain their power, as was argued in January 1983 by a group of intellectuals (including Chandra Muzaffar, Syed Husin Ali, and Goh Cheng Teik) at a seminar on "Modernization and National-Cultural Identity). But the general public did not appear to share this opinion. The perception of communal difference and communal competition still constituted a real barrier to unity. In this respect, and despite the emergence of the Malay middle class and weakening of the royal families, little had changed.

Communal competition was illustrated most dramatically by the 1969 riots. We have seen that they marked the failure of the policy of communal compromise, and led to a new generation of Malay leaders determined to enforce Malay dominance. During the months on which this monograph focusses, competition was demonstrated most commonly by disagreements over education policy and the implementation of the language policy in the education system, which will be discussed in the next chapter. The reasons why the symbolic issues raised in the legal system did not excite communal differences within the legal profession are examined in chapter three.

Proposals to reform the legal system were given impetus by the revival of interest in the notion of a national culture. In order to understand the political significance of these proposals, it is necessary to understand why national culture issues fell within the scope of national politics. It is generally the case in developing nations, and particularly in developing nations as heterogeneous as Malaya/Malaysia, that the government formulates an official expression of the culture and exploits it in nation building. Paradoxically, the greater the need for the unifying force that the culture represents, the greater the problems of reaching agreement on its characteristics. Nationalism exploits an idealised past when all members of the community supposedly shared the same culture and language in order to realise the ideal future of political and cultural unity. Fishman (1972) writes:

> Whereas traditionalism of various kinds seeks a return to or a preservation of the genuine past, nationalism seeks to "render the present a rational continuation of the past" (Bromage 1956, p. 29), indeed, it seeks and creates a usable past. (p.8)

In Malaysia, the communities lacked a common past, common religion, common language, common occupation, common artistic heritage—in all aspects, a common culture. Each community idealised its own past, but could not accept the ideal held by any other community as a model for future development. The non-Malays were placed under increasing pressures to accept the culture of the indigenous people as the framework of national ideology.

The notion of a national culture belongs within our discussion of the political context to the language policy because it demonstrates the Malays' drive to assert their dominance over the other communities. A national culture based on Malay values had originally been proposed by a meeting of Malay cultural organisations in December 1957. For the next thirteen years nothing was done to implement this.[14] It became a political issue only after the 1969 riots when the Government was obliged to take a tougher response to the problems of integrating the non-Malays into a Malay polity. In 1970, a national ideology, the *Rukunegara* (or "Articles of Faith in the State"—detailed in Andaya and Andaya 1982, p. 281) was proclaimed, and in the following year the First National Culture Congress established three principles. These were that

- the national culture should be based on the indigenous culture of the region;
- the features of other cultures must be suited to the national culture;
- Islam should be an important element of the national culture.

These three principles were symbolic of a desire for unity based on the preeminence of Malay culture. Nevertheless, they were sufficiently imprecise to permit different interpretations by different communities, depending on their own needs and concepts of culture. They made clear only that the national culture could not include any elements of the non-indigenous Chinese and Indian cultures that were considered inimicable to Malay culture. They did not spell out the criteria by which these elements were to be identified; nor did they state the process by which they might be assimilated, or the functions of a national culture. They did not make clear how far a national culture would be allowed to move away from the mainstream of traditional Malay culture. The Malay heartlands answered not at all and, as time went on, they increasingly interpreted the three principles as a political manifesto.

This ambiguity was complicated by the differences between the communities' cultures and their interpretations of the concept of culture. (See Abdullah Taib and Mohamed Yusoff Ismail, 1982 for socio-cultural differences.) Malay culture borrowed from Islam an ideal of how society should be organised and man's place within that society. It was a cooperative society that followed the principle of *gotong royong* (mutual help). The individual owed loyalty to his fellows and to his ruler, even under the most extreme circumstances. His conscience was bound by Islamic teaching and the need to satisfy his sense of *malu* (self respect). His notion of culture was essentially normative, and the norms were based on Islam. The Chinese community, on the other hand, belonged to a range of non-Islamic religious faiths. The Chinese valued his language because it represented his race and, more specifically, it bound him within his kinship structure. Intermarriage between different Chinese language groups was still relatively uncommon. He valued education both as a tool for strengthening his "face" and advancing himself and his family, and as a symbol of his cultural and artistic heritage. Whereas the Malay identified his traditional artefacts with the social relationships that they designated (see Winstedt 1947, revised in 1981, for a discussion of traditional Malay culture) the Chinese derived from his a sometimes overbearing pride in 4,000 years of recorded achievement. His approach to culture may be characterised as instrumental and descriptive rather than normative.

Before seeing how cultural differences generated communal antagonisms, it is essential first to examine the increased rigour with which Malay cultural values were applied within the Malay community. This rigour sprang from the perceived need to tighten unity within the Malay community. The pressures of change—of modernization, industrialization, urbanization, the growth of middle class, the worldwide resuscitation of Islam—were imposing severe strains on the traditional homogeneity of the Malay community, and hence on UMNO's political base. One academic identified five groups among the Malays, each taking a different stand on the cultural issue: "the iconoclasts" who rejected the realities of history and wanted a composite of all the ethnic cultures; "the conservative pro-bumis" such as the fundamentalists of PAS, who wanted a culture "based wholly and categorically on Malay culture and Islam"; the anglicized and westernized "secularists"; "the idealists," who espoused universal values and ignored political realities; and "the progressive nationalists," who followed official UMNO policy.[15] For example, PAS interpreted the Government's reliance on colonial institutions as a modernization based on shallow traditions and out of touch with the worldwide resurgence of Islam; and the new Malay middle class scorned the fundamentalists' refusal to acknowledge the new realities of the international economy. Moreover, economic policies designed to discriminate in favour of the Malays did not benefit all Malays equally and some groups—the new middle class—did considerably better than others—the rural poor. Hence the Government's attempts to deliver on the promises made after 1969 led to prosperity for some but also to disappointed expectations and exacerbated economic grievances. Many of the rural poor who benefited least belonged to conservative religious communities and were susceptible to the blandishments of PAS. These factors explain why UMNO politics were as often directed to holding the Malay community in line as to controlling the non-Malays. The administration worked hard to enforce Islamic orthodoxy. After the Batu Pahat incident, at which a gang of Muslim fanatics attacked a police station and killed and wounded a number of police personnel, religious practices which seemed likely to "disrupt the unity of the Malays" were condemned,[16] and more than fifty types of "deviant teachings" investigated.[17]

The administration's approach to the notion of a national culture was necessarily equivocal. Dr. Mahathir's attitude to the royal households was not as respectful as had been that of his predecessors, and this offended some Malay sensibilities. He based his power on the new urban Malay middle class whose feudal loyalties were weakening. But this class still represented a small percentage of the electorate, and the administration needed the support of the rural Malay vote. It took seriously the challenge offered by PAS (perhaps more seriously than PAS's actual electoral strength justified) and public announcements paid every respect to Islamic culture. On the other hand, it could not ignore the fact that almost fifty per cent of the population was non-Malay and non-Muslim, and could be led only by very small steps to espouse Malay values.

The Malay notion of culture and its implications for social behaviour provided the administration with tools for imposing control over the Malay community. For instance, in January 1983 Muslims were banned from working in the Genting Highlands Casino,[18] and were later banned from entering at all. In the same year, applicants for MARA (*Majlis Amanah Ra'ayat* or Council of Trust for the Indigenous People) loans had to sign a contract stating that they did not gamble, drink, or commit adultery, and priority was given to non-smokers.[19] These moves demonstrated to the Malay community that the administration took Islamic moral values seriously.

This enforcement of Malay culture within the Malay community was rigorously implemented through the religious courts. The administration agreed to extend the jurisdiction of Shariah Courts,[20] and to upgrade them to the level of Magistrates' Courts within the civil system in terms of administrative status and service.[21] (The implication seemed to be that Malays at least would have two choices of justice when they wished to pursue a case to court. And over time the authority of the Magistrates' system would be shared and correspondingly reduced.) Greater attention would be paid to regulations governing testimony and procedure.[22] "High level committees" were set up to plan a series of stages for introducing and implementing Islamic law more fully.[23] In different states laws were revised and penalties increased; for instance in Pahang

> Muslims found having sexual intercourse with non-Muslims shall be guilty of an offence and shall, on conviction, be liable to a fine not more than $1,000 or to imprisonment for a term not more than six months or both. (*New Straits Times*, 14 December 1982).[24]

Existing laws were enforced more rigorously. In Kota Baharu a Malay nurse was found guilty of committing *khalwat* (close physical proximity) with her driving instructor while parked in a brightly lit street outside her hospital and fined Malaysian $80. The court *kadi* commented that Muslim women in cars with men other than their husbands or relatives should sit at the back.[25]

Before 1969, there had appeared to be no question of the Malays imposing their cultural values on the non-Malays. Writing in 1965, Ratnam had restricted his concept of national culture to language

> since the Malays do not expect others to change their religions or even most of their social customs. (p. 71)

But the climate had changed, and in the new political conditions at the time of Dr. Mahathir's accession, Malay values were increasingly held out as desirable models for a national culture. The administration seemed at some points to favour persuading the non-Malays that the ideal Malay past constituted the only possible basis for a national culture and ideology. At other points it seemed to want to coerce acceptance and it veered increasingly towards the second option. The non-Malay position, that an ideal model might be fabricated from elements of all cultures, became steadily more defensive. The following example demonstrates this conflict between the communities fought over a symbolic issue in which neither side appeared to comprehend fully the other's concept of culture.

In November 1982 the Acting Culture, Youth, and Sports Minister (UMNO) ruled that the Chinese lion dance could not become part of the national culture.[26] This did not meant that the lion dance was banned—the Constitution guaranteed that every community might practice its own culture at its community functions[27] but that it would not be employed in official functions and ceremonies. The Acting Minister allowed that the dance was important to the Chinese but could not be recognised since the country as a whole did not accept it. (At about the same time the Ministry set up a Council to coordinate activities pertaining to silat, a Malay martial art of no interest to the non-Malays.)[28] He made the general point that the national culture, based on the three points agreed by the First National Culture Congress, would "eliminate racial cultures";[29] it might evolve or be created through legislation.

Direct responses followed from a spokesman for the President of the MCA,[30] the party's National Deputy Chairman,[31] and the Chairman[32] to the effect that the three principles should not be interpreted as the official concept of national culture, and that the First National Culture Congress was neither authoritative nor representative of every section of the national community. The notion of culture was associated with the artistic experience of a people, and must be permitted to evolve. A national culture should retain the best elements of all communal cultures, and could be neither legislated into existence nor expressed through legislation.

These arguments were answered first by a reminder of Dr. Mahathir's recent statement that the question of national culture based on the culture of the indigenous people should not arise anymore.[33] In succeeding chapters further examples are given of this imposition of a guillotine on contentious debates. The national culture belonged among those issues of which discussion apparently intended to arouse communal sensibilities was proscribed by the Sedition Act. The MCA had been party to the Act and was not about to endanger its relationship with UMNO by challenging the provisions of the Act.

The UMNO position on the national culture was amplified in a statement made by Anwar Ibrahim, soon to be minister of Culture, Youth, and Sports. He assured his audience that the cultures of the non-Malays would not be ignored "when a national culture is formulated." The national culture was intended to foster national unity and identity. He is quoted in the *Star* in January 1983 as stating:

> that to attain a national culture, there should be understanding, goodwill, and contacts among the various communities. "We must, then, build up a national attitude towards work ethics. When all the people, regardless of religion or background, follow this way of life, we would have achieved one point of contact," he said. "This point of contact is thus the key to achieve unity through a national identity," he stressed. Encik Anwar also said that the Government's efforts to inculate Islamic values into the peoples' way of life was also aimed to creating more contacts among people of all races.[34]

The UMNO case argued first by the Deputy Minister and then by Anwar Ibrahim may be summarised thus. Malaysia was still a country without a national identity. National identity was a function of a national culture which could be formulated and still had to be formulated. A national culture would embrace all aspects of the people's way of life including morality, and would be based on the three principles. How far it could evolve and how far it should be legislated into existence remained to be seen, but some legislation was probably necessary. Goodwill between the communities was a precondition both for the culture policy to succeed and for its desired end.

The lion dance was a particularly powerful symbol of Chinese culture and had previously aroused communal antagonisms (Milne and Mauzy 1980, p. 367). This episode demonstrated the extent of the disagreement over which strategy should be followed in order to create a national culture. The MCA argued for the evolution of a culture able to meet the needs of a multi-ethnic future; the notion that the past history of any one culture could provide a workable basis for this future was illusory. In Chinese terms, the Malay insistence on attempting to persuade, or failing that, coerce the non-Malays to accept the ideal Malay past as a model directly threatened their cultural and economic interests.

At several points in this monograph it is noted that the MCA elite placed high priority on maintaining its position within the Alliance. The lion dance incident shows that when they did express open disagreement with their senior partners in UMNO, they chose a symbolic rather than a practical issue. On this issue they represented their middle class constituents. The middle classes of all communities shunned open rivalry. In so short a time of gestation they were unlikely to shake off latent loyalties to their communal cultures, yet they were beginning to manifest a commonality of interest. (For latent and manifest cultures, see Becker and Geer 1960). They perceived that they had more to lose than gain from inter-communal conflict. They desperately feared a repeat of the 1969 riots. If the Alliance parties had clashed over communal issues of real economic and social importance, such as the quota system operated in tertiary education and the interpretation of constitutional guarantees to non-Malays, the social and economic differences among the elites of all three communities—and increasingly their middle classes on the one hand, and on the other the poor Malays, poor Chinese, and poor Indians—would have been dangerously exposed. But these masses still saw their interests in communal terms. For as long as the Alliance parties restricted their public political activities to debating symbolic rather than real differences, this state of affairs was likely to continue.

Islam is a missionary religion. The Malays based their culture on Islam and perceived it in normative terms. Hence they promoted it with missionary zeal, not only within their own community but increasingly within society at large. UMNO spoke for the Malays when it claimed that "Islam had the answers to the problems faced by the country.[35] A Morals Law was proposed, which would cover "all aspects of immorality, including prostitution, indecent exposure, obscene acts, and behavior."[36] Objections from non-Malays that the Law would infringe rights of privacy,[37] and that the morals lay outside the Government's rights to control were answered by the Government to the effect that "the proposed law was part of the Government' policy to expose elements of Islamic law to the people."[38]

This desire to bring about non-Malay acceptance of the Malay ideal marked a distinct breach with the policy followed by previous administrations. When in power, both Tunku Abdul Rahman and Datuk Hussein Onn had adhered to the line of administrative and cultural continuity. They now felt obliged to remind the new administration of the constitutional guarantees of Malaysia's official status as a secular state in which Islam was the state religion, and to warn against any attempt to make Malaysia an Islamic state against the wishes of one half the population.[39] Dr. Mahathir's interpretation of Islamic culture may have been bland compared to that made by PAS,[40] and may have been primarily intended to reassure the Malays of the administration's fidelity to first principles, but it frightened the non-Malays. In an interview with the *Far Eastern Economic Review* a spokesman for all non-Islamic religions in discussions over the proposed amendments to the Penal Code said

> when a Muslim talks about the national culture, you must remember that Islam makes no distinction among culture, politics, economics and religion—they are

> all one. That is why we are worried by the provision that all university students, irrespective of race or religion, must study Islamic civilization and history in Malaysia.[41]

The non-Malays perceive this Islamization as restricting their freedoms; the Malays saw it as an instrument for enhancing and broadening concepts of nationalism adopted from the materialistic West.[42]

The suggested Islamic culture syllabus[43] was shelved. But, as in the case of the Morals Law, the pressure to drop the proposal came from outside the Government and not from either of the two major parties representing the interests of the non-Malays. The imposition of Malay culture reinforced the pressures imposed by Malay political and economic privileges. Culture policy constituted an arm of political and economic policy, and the social affects could not always be distinguished. It seemed that every time the non-Malays were close to fulfilling the conditions for integration and equal partnership, the Malays erected yet another hurdle (Goh Cheng Teik, 1983, p. 10). For instance, it had been suggested several times that the script of the national language be changed to *Jawi* (Arabic) script rather than the usual *Rumi* (Romanised form). *Jawi* street signs were proposed.[44] Such a hurdle would not delay the non-Malays for long. Immigrant people able to master Malay at least as well as the Malays were perfectly capable of expressing it in a further, relatively straightforward script. Nevertheless, this proposal helps explain the sense of insecurity of which the non-Malays complained.[45]

This chapter first considered the importance of language planning in Malaysia. The main characteristics of the legal system at the time of the Directive were introduced. The political and cultural context was examined, and it was shown why conflicts in defining and implementing a culture policy had political significance. Succeeding chapters will demonstrate that this context generated the drive for reform of the legal system with the switch to Malay as the medium of the law as a first step.

Unlike many of her neighbours in the region, Malaya/Malaysia did not have to fight for freedom. The early leaders had no good reason to scrap the administrative machinery bequeathed them by the colonial power, and every reason to apply it to their own ends. However, the period of time with which this monograph is concerned witnessed a new determination to create the national identity and unity that other countries had appeared to achieve in the wake of revolution. The new administration chose this path partly because of its own ideological leaning, and partly in response to the political, social, and communal forces that first manifested themselves in 1969.

Chapter 2 deals with the influence that these forces had on language planning in the education system. Chapter 3 discusses their influence on legal policy and language policy in the legal system.

CHAPTER TWO

The Politics of Language Policy

The national language policy was developed in order to bring about the use of Malay as the official and national language. It has a lengthy history, rent with contradictions, and illustrates many of the general points that we have just examined. The policy predated Independence and was fostered by at least some sections of the colonial administration. Its implementation constituted the most serious attempt made by post-Independence administrations to create national unity. It could be fully realised only when applied throughout the range of national institutions. Its extension from the education system to the legal system was always promised, yet difficulties in converting the education system to Malay medium always served as a convenient excuse for delay.

For as long as the policy was extended and developed throughout the schools and universities, the obligation to enforce the gradual use of Malay was met. By 1981 the achievement of a Malay medium educational system was in sight, but the ideals of national unity and identity based on a common language were (in the eyes of many) no closer to fulfillment. The non-Malays and foreign investors still enjoyed economic dominance, and language policy had paradoxically provided a new focus to communal competition. This chapter looks at how language policy reflected the political and cultural developments we have already noted, and concludes by examining some of the factors that made implementation within the legal system an attractive next step.

In Malaysia language and education policies were often synonymous. The language policy was always intended to be applied in a range of activities —street advertising, the armed forces, Parliament, the bureaucracy, and of course, the law. But by far the greatest attention was paid to the education system. Education policy focused on propagating the use of Malay through national and national-type schools, and then through Malay-medium universities. It then focused on increasing the number of places available, in particular to Malays, at all levels. In practice, this meant that progressively more pupils and students were exposed to a Malay-medium education. In most other respects, education policy only slightly modified the models set by the colonial administration and by the educational system in Britain. For instance, in 1980, final year school pupils still sat the Cambridge University Local Higher School Certificate (HSC). Professor Diraja

Ungku Aziz, Universiti Malaya Vice Chancellor, made the case for keeping the examination system as it was except that the papers would be translated.

> "It's the continuity we want. We know them (Cambridge), they know us. We could go into other systems, but it would be more difficult. Cambridge is already accepted here and abroad."[1]

We have noted the old colonial policy of encouraging communal cooperation among the elites and of separating the masses. This was maintained by the colonial educational system. The English-medium schools taught up to British university entrance and were attended by members of the Malay royal houses and those other Malays earmarked for posts within the colonial administration, wealthy Chinese, and a very few wealthy Indians. English was thus marked as the language of privilege, prosperity, and modernity. Mandarin-medium schools taught at elementary and secondary levels, and Malay and Tamil schools at primary levels only. When the mood changed and the decision was taken to integrate the communities, this was also reflected in education policy. In 1950 the Barnes Committee reported that Malay should be the common political denominator, and that a predominantly Malay-medium primary school system should be employed as the tool to build up Malayan nationalism. The unease shown by the Chinese obliged their leaders to commission the Fenn-Wu Report (1951), which urged far greater autonomy for Chinese schools. The British permitted the Chinese their say, then quietly shrugged off the Report's more radical proposals. They correctly assessed that in any last resort the MCA would always choose to honour its contract with UMNO. Agreement on the preeminence of the Malay language and the protection of Chinese and Indian cultures was one of the few positive achievements of the Communities Liaison Committee (1950). The Reid Commission's decision that Malay and English should share the status of official languages for ten years, after which English would lose this status, was endorsed by the Constitution. The ten-year grace period was intended to be used in developing Malay language textbooks, terminologies, and translations. (Vikor 1983, p. 63).

In 1956 the Razak Report proposed the formation of a national school system in which Malay and English were to be compulsory subjects in all primary and secondary schools. The proposal was adopted by the Education Ordinance of 1957. This distinguished between primary schools which taught in Malay and were classified as national schools, and primary schools which taught in some other language but in which Malay and English were compulsory and were classified as national-type schools. The development of alternative systems was discouraged by the regulation that only schools that chose to convert to the national and national-type systems were able to make a claim upon state funds. The Rahman Talib Report (1960) recommended, and the Education Ordinance of 1961 extended, the systems to secondary schools.

The western-educated elites of the Alliance perhaps lacked personal commitment to the language policy, but they now owed their political careers to their masses and no longer to the colonial administration. As the ten-year deadline of 1967 approached, the UMNO leaders were made increasingly aware that the promises of the Constitution could not be evaded. In the 1964 elections the Alliance had diverted public attention to the Confrontation with Indonesia and PMIP's internal difficulties, and won a healthy majority. But the communal and social problems had not been addressed, and the apparent demonstration of support for the administration's policies was illusory. The National Language Act (1967) made belated recognition of the underlying Malay discontent. It had the ostensive purpose of unifying the population on the basis of Malay language, and made the single most important move in that direction until that time (Roff M. 1967). Malay was established as the only language that could claim official usage as a right; all other languages, including English, would be used only where convenient (Enloe 1967, p. 207). Like the Directive, the Act laid down the ground rules for implementing language policy, but allowed room for different interpretations to be made in different circumstances.

A time table was set for using Malay as the medium of instruction throughout national schools, and throughout national-type schools except for classes in the mother tongue and English. But the ten-year grace period had not been well spent and preparations were inadequate for a rapid transition. The switch would only be made very gradually. In 1968 local studies, music, art, and physical education in Standards one, two, and three were taught in Malay in the national schools. English was taught as a compulsory second language and had the official status of the "second most important language" (Asmah Haji Omar 1979, p. 24). The Act took up the recommendation of the Razak Report for teaching the Pupils' Own Language (POL) in national schools when this was neither Malay nor English and when at least fifteen pupils requested it. In practice this was limited to Mandarin, Tamil, Iban (in Sarawak), and Kadazan (in Sabah) (ibid., p. 26). Thus it could be claimed that the languages of the non-Malays were protected. Based on this condition, the non-Malay parties had agreed to the constitution.

At first the Act seemed adequate. The non-Malays hoped to impose restrictions on the notion of "official usage," but they always accepted the principle of a national language. The majority of Malays seemed to be appeased. But the 1969 election and subsequent rioting demonstrated the underlying insecurity. UMNO was obliged to insist on a reformulation of the constitutional contract between the three communities in favour of the Malays, and to take the issues of language and social development rather less than for granted. The timetable for using Malay as the medium of instruction was confirmed. Beginning in 1970, most Standard 1 subjects were to be taught in Malay in national-type schools. In the next year, Standard 2 would follow suit, and so on until 1982

(1983 in Sabah and Sarawak) when all primary and secondary levels would be Malay medium.

The degree of coincidence between the education and language policies has been noted. Hence, the achievement of the 1982 target for an all Malay-medium education system represented a major success in administering the language policy. Next we will examine to what extent the implementation of the education/ language policy brought about the sense of common identity that the nation's leaders had strived for so long to assert.

In the eyes of the Malays, the ideal of a "just society" (Wilson 1977, p. 62) could be achieved only when they had overcome their economic backwardness in relation to the non-Malays, in particular the Chinese. This economic gap was the crucial obstacle to national integration (Chandriah Appa Roo, et al. 1977, p. 77). In other words, an integrated Malaysian nation was to be based on a Malay nationalism that offered conditional "accommodation" (Ratnam 1965, p. 26) to the non-Malays. The conditions included acceptance of the principles governing the NEP. This involved accepting educational discrimination, and particularly in areas of scientific and technical education. Society was able to assimilate only so many graduates in Malay studies, literature, and history—the areas of study treated most comprehensively by the rural schools still attended mostly by Malays, approximately 80 per cent of whom still lived in kampongs. The typical Malay graduate found employment back in the school system or in the civil service (about 80 per cent Malay in 1981)[2] but not in industry which placed greater value on scientific or technological qualifications. Policy at the tertiary level therefore paid particular attention to creating a class of Malay science graduates.

In 1970, Malays made up only 1.3 per cent of the total enrollment in tertiary level engineering, 12.4 per cent in science, and 17.2 per cent in medicine. By 1975 the numbers had increased to 31.9 per cent, 25.8 per cent, and 39.1 per cent respectively.[3] Between 1966 and 1975 the MARA Institute of Technology (reserved for Malays) produced nearly 3,000 graduates (Milne and Mauzy 1970, 1980, p. 331) mostly of undergraduate certificate and diploma courses. In 1976 Universiti Malaya set up an *Assasi Sains* or Basic Science program to prepare Malay school graduates for entry into undergraduate science faculties.

UMNO's Malay constituency had greatly resented the use of English at the tertiary level, both as the language of the classroom and of the library, and the advantages of this for the non-Malay students. After 1969 Malay increasingly replaced English, at least in the classroom. Universiti Kebangsaan Malaysia (UKM) had used Malay since its inception and Universiti Pertanian Malaysia (UPM) since June 1983. In 1981, Universiti Sains Malaysia (USM) taught all arts and humanities and 80 per cent of science subjects in Malay.[4] This was done at least in theory; in practice, many USM lecturers continued to use English in defiance of the regulations.[5] All first year courses in the five universities were planned to be taught in Malay for the first time in 1983.[6]

By 1983, the statistics provided evidence for arguing that the declared aims of the policy had been successfully achieved. A newspaper concluded an article published to celebrate the twenty-fifth anniversary of Independence thus:

> After 25 years, the Government's most notable achievement is the introduction of a common language, Bahasa Malaysia, which has been accepted by all races, and is used as a medium of instruction from primary to university levels.
>
> With every child being exposed to the national language in school, communication among the races will cease to be a problem as they become more and more proficient in the language. This will be an important factor in national integration and unity.[7]

The first paragraph is unexceptional; the second rather more problematic. It reflects the ideology of national unity that had been created for consumption by non-Malays as much as Malays. However, a number of the flies in the ointment seemed to show that implementation of the policy had failed in this objective, and perhaps had even caused the rifts between the communities to widen, (a view held by the DAP at least). The DAP argued this as a matter of policy, and even some prominent Malays acknowledged the extent of racial differences.[8]

The MCA elite had been able to sell the constitutional agreement and the subsequent legislation to their community by virtue of the relationship that they enjoyed with the leaders of UMNO and their pretentions to a "national" role (Wang Gungwu 1981, pp. 232-48). But the price they paid for accepting Malay demands was a loss of ideological independence. Except for a brief period in 1959, this relationship with UMNO was consistent. In 1980, the MCA Vice Chairman explained to an election meeting that

> The most important reality is that real power is in the hands of UMNO due to a combination of historical circumstances, and thinking that it can be otherwise is being wishful. . . . Datuk Lew said the Chinese must change their attitude of protest to an attitude of cooperation. Casting your votes for the opposition parties like the DAP is proof of this protest mentality, which is the result of not fully appreciating the realities.[9]

The MCA elite had persuaded their rank and file that in exchange for agreeing to education and economic policies which discriminated in favour of the Malays, they had won guarantees of citizenship and protection of Chinese culture and language. As time went on, the support became grudging as the continued electoral interest in the DAP and Gerakan showed. First, the MCA leaders appeared to be divided among themselves. In an interview with the party Chairman, a columnist commented

> In the MCA the factions have got so strong and your fights have gone from small factions to the leadership.
>
> It is becoming a laughing stock when you talk of uniting the Chinese. You are

> fighting for the unity of the Chinese while the Chinese leaders are quarreling among themselves. How can the Chinese support such a party?[10]

Second, the ideal of separate Chinese development represented by the Mandarin-educated leaders both inside and outside the MCA continued to exert a powerful fascination, as we shall see when we turn to the Chinese education movement. Third, the compromise between educational and economic policies on the one hand and communal relationships on the other had been posed in terms that made the Chinese extremely sensitive to any apparent renegotiation of the bargain. They were constantly reminded that they had paid the price. Differentials between Chinese and Malay per capita incomes were less obvious to the non-Malay in the street than were the signs of economic discrimination. Two examples make the point. Almost all transport licenses were held by Malays.[11] Therefore when a Chinese caught a taxi he could be almost certain that the owner of record was a Malay, whatever the racial identities of the capital holder—who might well be Chinese—and, more immediately, of the driver. And, a typical property advertisement for houses on a new estate offered "5% discount to Bumiputras"[12] (sons of the soil). On the other hand, there were good reasons for wondering whether the UMNO elite intended to keep their side of the bargain.

Non-Malays' worry about the long-term future of their communities was fed by a number of incidents which seemed to reflect continued Malay antagonism to their presence. At one extreme, on 16 October 1980 a gang of Islamic fanatics assaulted the Batu Pahat police station; this was later rumoured to have been intended as a first strike before an attack on Chinese traders in the market. Less shocking but perhaps more serious in its implications was the speech made in Parliament in 1978 by an UMNO MP, Mark Koding demanding the closure of Chinese and Indian schools in order to implement the national language policy. In the subsequent trial under the Sedition Act (1970), his counsel argued that he was only quoting from *The Malay Dilemma,* a book that had earned the incoming Prime Minister, Dr. Mahathir, an early reputation for Malay extremism. The judge commented

> If it was true that the accused was quoting from *The Malay Dilemma* which is much stronger, then the accused's speech was not serious and he should be acquitted.[13]

Mr. Koding was found guilty. But the anxiety raised by such incidents could not so easily be dispelled.

More damaging, however, was the impact of events in implementing the language policy for which the Government was directly responsible. Two examples are the long-running unease over the implementation of POL classes and the controversy that surrounded the implementation of the "3Rs" syllabus.

The concern among the non-Malays that the Government was not abiding by the guarantees of support for the non-Malay cultures is demonstrated by suspicions that the teaching of Pupils's Own Languages in national schools was declining.[14] According to one critic, POL programmes suffered chiefly from a shortage of qualified teachers. Those who did teach the subjects were often recruited at the last minute, and were overworked and underpaid.[15] Government spokesmen either denied all such allegations or argued, as did the Deputy Education Minister, (an MCA member, Dr. Tan Tiang Hong), that responsibility for organising and teaching the programmes rested with head teachers and not with the Ministry.[16] But the complaints did not die away. The same points were taken up in a Memorandum signed by 226 Chinese and 20 Indian literary, educational, and cultural organisations. They argued that permanent POL teachers be appointed in order to avoid dislocation caused by part-time teachers; classes be made compulsory and not relegated to Saturday mornings; schools keep parents informed of POL programmes; and that a senior Ministry of Education official be given responsibility for all programmes. This, coupled with a reference to the guarantees proposed by the Razak Report, was clearly directed at the Deputy Minister, and by extension, the MCA.[17]

This POL Memorandum suggested that the Government was not performing its statutory duties. The opposition to the "3Rs" policy arose from a suspicion that the Government was actively attempting to suppress the cultures of the non-Malays. The policy aimed to simplify the national and national-type primary school curricula, but was thought to be aimed at converting the national-type schools into Malay medium national schools by covert means. An earlier statement by the Ministry of Education had apparently suggested that Chinese and Indian national-type primary schools were not going to be affected by any curriculum changes.[18] The controversy was sparked by the realisation that these schools would indeed be involved, and by the Ministry's "inept handling of the issues."[19] In particular, the first edition of all teacher material (except for the teaching of Mandarin, Tamil, and English) was published in Malay,[20] and to many this seemed the thin end of the all-Malay-medium wedge.

The MCA leaders moved quickly to keep control of their community. The party President was reported to have stated that

> The 3R system as it is being implemented in Chinese schools is an insult to the MCA and is unacceptable to the party . . . . I wish to reiterate that the MCA will sink or swim with Chinese primary schools.[21]

Strong words that would seem to position the party in confrontation with its senior partner in the Government. But they were coupled with the promise that the MCA "will not capitalise on the issue politically."[22]

At first sight, the notion that the MCA could contest a move to make Chinese national-type schools Malay medium throughout and enforce their conversion to the national system without applying political means appears to be contradictory. But the concept of a "political issue" was limited. In practice, it referred to any dispute that actually, or potentially, infringed the Sedition Act and the restrictive legislation introduced after 1969.

Its relative failure to bring out the Malay constituency in the May 1969 elections and the racial riots that followed had taught UMNO an important lesson. Paternalism and a delicate concern to balance the claims of the different communities were no longer adequate. Large numbers of Malays had abstained or voted for opposition parties to teach UMNO a lesson, and the party seemed to have been massively betrayed by its Chinese allies. Evidently, communal animosities could not be so easily dissipated; and so they had to be contained. Despite attempts to "restore normalcy" (Von Vorys 1976, p. 345), nothing would be the same again. Dr. Mahathir was among those UMNO leaders who had lost his seat. He represented those determined to pursue Malay interests with greater vigour than before, and with considerably less regard to the interests of the non-Malays. The Sedition Act was one of the tools chosen to enforce the new arrangement.

The Act restricted the arena for acceptable political debate to issues that did not challenge Malay rights, the communal status quo, and, by implication, the relationship between the governing communal parties. It had helped foster the notion that the non-Malay parties could advance only in lock-step with UMNO.[23] In the 1982 "3Rs" controversy, the MCA reflected this notion when its leaders promised to go on searching for a compromise formula with UMNO, but in private. Above all else, the party would continue to avoid issues which might inflame communal tensions. The DAP was regularly attacked by the National Front parties for breaking this convention, and for using the language issue in order to attain its own political aims and to further separate the communities.

> The members make language a political issue at every general election, and wherever they do so, they lose badly.[24]

The MCA's fear of communal tensions reflected not only high moral purpose but sensible self-interest. Even before 1969 many Chinese had distrusted the party's role of conciliator, perhaps even appeaser. The riots resulted in part from Chinese frustration and demonstrations following the defeat of the MCA at the hands of the DAP within the Chinese constituencies. In the event of further conflict, the pattern might be repeated.

It was clearly in the interests of UMNO that the MCA should retain a hold over the Chinese community. This time they got their junior partners off the hook by issuing a Ministry of Education statement to the effect that a misunderstanding had arisen over the Malay language teaching guide, and that this was the "root cause" of the controversy.[25] The guide was intended as a sample only; nowhere did it state that teachers should teach in Malay. The medium of instruction remained unchanged, and teachers should prepare their own materials. The impracticality of providing teaching materials in one language for classes to be taught in another did not receive comment (although teachers were later reported to be overburdened by the extra work involved).[26] The Ministry later announced that teaching aids and instructions would also be produced in Mandarin and Tamil, and these would not be merely translations of the Malay medium aids.[27] The MCA had accepted the political realities and contented itself by insisting that moral education in Chinese national-type schools should reflect Chinese values.

The MCA also demanded that the time given to teaching English be increased,[28] and eventually won a concession that the language be taught one year earlier than originally planned.[29] Whether or not an extra year of primary school English can make much difference is debatable. This seemed intended as a sop to that middle-class section of the Chinese community that had themselves been educated in English and were most conscious of the economic and political advantages that accrued to mastery of an international language in addition to the national language.

There were grounds for supposing that throughout the school system standards of English teaching were declining.[30] This was usually explained by the lack of trained teachers.[31] It was a matter for official regret, but regret quietly voiced; the Government was taking two lines on English teaching and these were apparently contradictory. On the one hand, the national elite—and in particular the Malay elite—must be encouraged to include English in their arsenal of languages, and no doubt the protestations of continued support for English teaching were made in good faith.[32] But the masses—and in particular the non-Malay masses— must be directed away from English culture and towards the goal of a Malay-speaking polity. The emphasis differed depending on the audience; to the one, "English is the second language and essential for international dealings"—a line adopted by members of the elder generation of the Malay leadership who may themselves have been educated in English.[33] And to the other, "English is the second language but Malay is the national language and pre-eminent."[34] The second was intended for general domestic consumption. With some hesitation, and after 1969 with increasing certainty, the Government argued that Malay should be developed as a major factor for national unity—a very different course than the one followed in Singapore, for instance, where lip service was paid to the notion of a national language but in practice English was adopted as the language of modernization. The differences in official attitudes of the two countries are demonstrated by the overt recruitment drive conducted by the Singaporean Government for British judges to servein the High Court. Government spokesmen explained that local advocates either lacked expertise or earned too much from private practice to be interested.[35] So in this case—and certainly not generally, for Singapore's policy on recruiting foreign expertise has not blown hot and cold—quality was considered more important than nationality or a knowledge of the local context.

There were signs that university students at least were expected to take seriously the notion of English as the second most important language. Universiti Malaya collaborated with the British Council and Birmingham University on the

Universiti Malaya English for Special Purposes Project, (1975-80) and then with the British Council alone on the Universiti Malaya Spoken English Project (1980-83). How much effect these projects could have in the long run was debatable. The political and economic systems made a knowledge of Malay an essential prerequisite for upward mobility, but offered only the small high-flying minority the incentive to add specialized English to their other language skills. The electoral threat posed on the east coast by the resurgent fundamentalist PAS and domestic political considerations meant that encouragement given to English should be discreet, and it could never be seen to gain at the expense of Malay.

The DAP claimed to support the concept of a simplified "3Rs" syllabus,[36] but opposed the form in which it was to be implemented. Firstly, the time was not right; most teachers in the national-type schools were not sufficiently fluent in Malay and most of the books under the new syllabus were in that medium.[37] This argument neatly rings the changes on the case put up against the implementation of language policy in the courts, that lawyers were not sufficiently fluent and almost all the necessary documentation was in English. Secondly, it would harm the integrity of the Chinese and Indian cultures. This was quite consistent with the party's policy that all the communities' main languages and cultures should share official status,[38] and the appeal made by all non-Malay opposition parties since Independence (Roff, W. R. 1974). Thirdly, DAP claimed that the syllabus would damage educational standards, particularly in arithmetic.[39] In an apparent attempt to divide the MCA leadership from their supporters, they cabled the MCA, the MIC, and two smaller National Front Parties, Gerakan and Sarawak United Peoples Party (SUPP), inviting them to form a united front against implementation of the "3Rs" system.[40] Despite continued worries expressed by Chinese guilds,[41] the MCA leadership were not to be drawn. The Party President remarked of the DAP's offer

> We will tackle the problem in our own way and we will not capitalise on important issues like this. This is the difference between us and the DAP.[42]

This supports our description of the MCA leadership style—an avoidance of any stance that might imply confrontation with their senior partners and a liking for closed-door negotiations at Government level. By suggesting that MCA and DAP politics differed most significantly in style (and, by implication, political maturity), Datuk Lee San Choon appeared to recognise that the DAP had touched a political nerve. The relationship that the MCA elite enjoyed with their UMNO colleagues was always tempered by the need to retain support among the Chinese electorate, which meant considerable attention was paid to trying to enforce party loyalty at branch level.

The DAP had spoken of the possible effects on not only Chinese but also Indian schools, and had initially appealed to the MIC to join its proposed united front. That these overtures were rejected must have surprised no one. While the MCA was still searching its conscience, the MIC embraced the policy; it would "not have anything to do with the cable" sent by the DAP.[43] The party was in no condition to go out on a limb and risk conflict with its senior National Front partner. Preoccupied with the internecine feuding and personality conflicts that had cursed it since its inception,[44] it was ineffectual. In 1981, the party president calculated that of the 1.3 million Indians in the country, only 560,000 were working and 235,000 were party members.[45] This latter figure looks comparatively healthy when compared to the size of the community, but not in terms of the total electorate. The Malaysian Hindu Council complained about the apparent lack of provisions made for teaching POL classes within the "3Rs" curriculum.[46] But otherwise those sections of the Indian community not already bespoken by the opposition followed the MIC line.[47] The clarification made by the Minister of Education that teachers of national-type schools were to continue teaching in their own languages was welcomed, and so were the subsequent statements by the Prime Minister.

Dr. Mahathir reiterated that the constitutional guarantees to continue vernacular education were clear, and that the Government did not intend to abandon the language of any one community.[48] The "3Rs" syllabus should in no way be seen as a covert attempt to draw national-type schools into the national system and the Government would not act to convert a school unless specifically asked to do so. The relevant clause in the Education Act (Clause 21(2)) was only "an enabling clause."[49] But promises were obviously not enough, and he went further.

> There are some leaders in certain quarters who are making an issue out of this. The Government will take action if they continue and if they incite racial dissatisfaction and conflict. He also accused certain quarters of promoting the misunderstanding over the 3R education system "to create dissatisfaction and uneasiness among the Chinese." I would like to remind them that there are certain things which are sensitive to not only the Malays but the Chinese and Indians as well. They cannot be discussed as they lead to racial problems.[50]

The "leaders in certain quarters" were clearly the leaders of the DAP. This statement also warned Gerakan, which was badly split on the issue,[51] and the MCA rank and file to stay in line. The warning was repeated a week later by the Deputy Prime Minister.[52] The MCA and MIC joined their senior partner in anathematizing the activities of those who "were using children to serve their own political interests"[53]—a considerable turnabout since the days of the Barnes Report (1951), the Fenn Wu Report (1951), and the Razak Report (1956), when educational issues had been the staple of Malaysian politics. Now, political dissent on educational matters was associated with racial propaganda, and the threat to apply the Sedition Act was clear. Threats of the use of extraordinary powers against opposition parties and individuals who had seemed about to go "too far" have been noted before in Malaysia's history (see Means 1976, p. 413). But this time the argument was posed in racial terms that demonstrated the fissures still dividing the mass of the population. Unless the non-Malays buckled to, then the Malays in the form of UMNO and the Government would exact reparations. The will to apply drastic measures was demonstrated by the use of the Internal Security (Prohibition of Documents) (No. 5) Order 1982 to ban a document entitled "3R and the Dilemma of the Non-Malay Students" written by a DAP MP, V. David.[54] And after these warnings, the debate over the "3Rs" syllabus petered away in a prolonged grumble over whether it actually worked and how sufficient additional teachers might be recruited and trained in order to lessen the workload.[55]

The POL and "3Rs" controversies show that the non-Malays felt threatened by the Government's failure to support their cultures and languages, and by its apparent embarkation on a policy intended to actively suppress their culture and languages. In neither case did the chief political parties representing the non-Malays associate themselves with marked enthusiasm with their communities. But if National Front politics did not provide any panacea to educational problems, non-political avenues were open, at least to those who could afford private education. The non-Malays and, in particular, the middle-class Chinese voted with their feet. This point may be illustrated by looking first at the independent Chinese schools, and then at the exodus of students to universities overseas.

The 1961 Education Ordinance had given private vernacular schools the option of joining the national or national-type education systems and thereby keeping Government subsidies, or of not joining the system and financing themselves. It tightened up the provisions of the 1957 Educational Ordinance, and one clause (21/2) apparently gave the Ministry of Education the power to convert national-type schools into national schools at his discretion. This was controversial; it attacked the right to education in one's mother tongue, which was guaranteed by the Constitution and was particularly dear to the hearts of those Chinese educated in Mandarin and without ties to the English-educated Malay elite. Despite the financial penalties involved in remaining outside the national or national-type systems, 17 of the then 69 Chinese secondary schools elected to stay independent.[56] The private school movement did not fade away; on the contrary, it grew. By 1982 the number of independent Chinese secondary schools had risen to 60, of which 37 were in Peninsular Malaysia and 23 in Sabah and Sarawak. In 1975 they organised their own Unified Examinations Board and syllabuses and textbooks to teach to the requirements of the Board. In December 1980,[57] 8,466 students sat the Board's examinations, and between 1976 and 1982 the pupil population rose from 32,000 to 44,600.[58] This demonstrated significant dissatisfaction with the national and national-type school systems and with the implementation of the national language policy. Such dissatisfaction was perhaps typical of post-colonial societies in that it showed suspicion that an indigenous system must necessarily be defective, designed only to boost the superiority of one community and not up to international standards. The degree of support that these independent schools commanded within the Chinese community was further indicated by the value of donations and contributions made to cover annual deficits—between 1975 and 1980, a total of Malaysian $32 million;[59] and in 1982, on average Malaysian $200,000 per school.[60]

The support for the free schools came in part from loyalty to Chinese culture and perhaps a retreat to certain aspects of that culture. The Chinese seemed to be losing hopes of effecting political solutions to their problems, certainly through the medium of the MCA.[61] They were accepting the role of "resident stranger" (McVey, ms. 1983, p. 18). They were prepared to master the national language, but looked for compensation in their own businesses and own religions.[62] They were also turning to their own educational system. There were sound economic reasons why a middle-class family might risk the apparent disadvantages and send their children to an independent school.

Although a pupil received most of his schooling in Mandarin, he gained a fair grasp of Malay and English. His Unified Examination Board certificate was not officially recognised in Malaysia but was quite acceptable to some universities in the United Kingdom, Australia, New Zealand, United States, Canada, and most important, Taiwan. Taiwanese university education 0as cheap—only about Malaysian $500 per month.[63] Again, a Taiwanese degree certificate had no official validity. But particularly if in business studies or engineering, it might be most attractive to Chinese-owned companies.

Nevertheless, the number of Malaysians studying in Taiwan constituted only a small percentage of those who had left for education overseas. In order to understand where the language policy was not successful in promoting its objectives of national unity and economic justice, we need to look a little more carefully at university education.

Figures demonstrate the increase in university enrollments, particularly among the Malays. In 1963 the one university (Universiti Malaya, founded in Singapore in 1949) had a total enrollment of 1,736 of whom only 20.6 per cent were Malay. The Government responded to the 1969 riots by drastically increasing the number of places, and the Malays benefited disproportionately. In 1970, the three universities had a total enrollment of 8,148. In 1975, all tertiary courses including degree, diploma, certificate, and pre-university courses enrolled 31,532 students. (The 1980 total of 77,916 given in the Fourth Malaysia Plan is not strictly comparable since it excludes pre-university students but includes those studying abroad.)[64] These figures break down among the communities as follows.

	1963	1970	1975
Malays	358 (20.6%)	3,235 (39.7%)	20,525 (65.1%)
Chinese	1,050 (60.5%)	4,009 (49.1%)	9,809 (31.1%)
Indians	286 (16.5%)	595 (7.3%)	1,040 (3.3%)
Others	42 (2.4%)	309 (3.8%)	158 (0.5%)
Total	1,736 (100%)	8,148 (100%)	31,532 (100%)

Of the 5,501 first year students enrolled in the five universities in 1980, 3,427 (62.3%) were Malay.[65]

University places were awarded to the communities on a quota basis. Precise figures for the quotas are difficult to obtain. Gullick (1981) gives 44 per cent as the intended proportion of Malays which would be achieved in 1983 (p. 240), but this seems to be an underestimation. The proportion of Malays had been allowed to grow considerably; in 1980 it reached 62.3 per cent of that year's intake.[66] Later that year the Minister of Education announced that the percentage difference would be gradually reduced by two per cent each year, and suggested that Malays should make up 55 per cent of the total and non-Malays 45 per cent.[67] Some UMNO members wanted to defer even this modest increased intake of non-Malays on the basis that it would undermine efforts to raise the educational and economic standards of the Malays.[68] But according to the DAP an increase of this proportion amounted to only an additional 30-40 non-Malay students each year.[69]

Against this increase in enrollments must be set the fact that the universities were not filling their places; for instance, in 1981 Universiti Malaya had enrolled fewer students than its capacity of 10,000, and Universiti Kebaangsan Malaysia had room for another 2,000.[70] So the percentage of non-Malay enrollments was allowed to shrink even when Malays did not fill their quota.

But the demand for tertiary education by non-Malays had not decreased. On the contrary, it had massively increased. It is true that while local universities had almost doubled their intake between 1978 and 1980 the actual number of applicants dropped. In 1978, 23,000 eligible applicants applied for places and in 1980, only 12,735. However, at the same time the number of Malaysians going abroad for tertiary education had grown out of all proportion. The figure cited most often in 1981 was 40,000,[71] of whom less than one third were government-sponsored.

The largest number went to the United Kingdom—up from 1,713 in 1969 to 12,850 in 1977, (but despite the apparent precision of these figures, no one seemed to know for certain).[72] They reached a peak of about 17,000 (including school pupils) in 1980.[73] Other beneficiaries were Australia (in 1980, about 6,000), India (6,000), Canada (5,000), the United States (4,000), New Zealand, and Singapore.[74] Only the ablest travelled on Government scholarships and most of these were Malay. Of the self-supported majority, perhaps four-fifths were Chinese. (Gullick 1981, p. 232.)

The implication becomes clear when we note the discrepancy between the proportion of Malays in local science faculties and the proportion in the professions. We have seen that by 1975 Malays constituted 31.9 per cent, 25.8 per cent, and 35.1 per cent of their tertiary level classes in engineering, science and medicine. Yet in 1979 they made up only 11 per cent of professional architects, 11.6 per cent of engineers, and 8.6 per cent of doctors. Hence the number of non-Malays who qualified abroad and came back to practise greatly outweighed the increase in Malay enrollments in Malay medium local universities.

The sincerity of the Government in its avowed intention to protect vernacular schools within the national-type system and its grudging toleration of the independent Chinese schools were always in doubt. But there was no mistaking its determination to prevent the development of an independent Chinese tertiary education movement. Plans by a private company, massively supported by 4,238 Chinese Guilds and Associations,[75] to establish a mainly Chinese medium university (Merdeka University) were contested up to the Federal Court. The appellants claimed that the educational policy of using Malay as the medium of instruction violated Constitutional guarantees given to the use of other languages (Article 152) and the rights of Chinese citizens in education (Article 8). The appellants lost and the Government won a ban on any further appeal to the Privy Council in London.[76]

The policy of positive discrimination in favour of the Malays meant that opportunities for advancement of non-Malays at the tertiary level had to be sharply curtailed, so far as that was politically expedient. At home, this meant not only banning the establishment of Merdeka University, but limiting the growth of even the national university system. The DAP argued for establishing up to five new universities;[77] and at the time of writing, plans for one more are still being considered (but with little official enthusiasm). When set against the estimated annual Malaysian $500 million spent in foreign capital to support students in overseas universities,[78] the estimated cost of at least Malaysian $100 million to set up a university and $30 million a year to maintain one with a student population of 2,000 may not be excessive over time.[79] But it is questionable whether there was a sufficient number of qualified Malays in proportion to non-Malays on the existing quota system to populate a further university.

Thus far we have seen that the number of enrollments at local universities increased massively after 1969, that most of this increase was taken up by Malay enrollments, and that the number of non-Malay remained more or less static. Meanwhile, the number of applicants had actually declined. But on the other hand, applications to and enrollments in overseas English-speaking universities went up by leaps and bounds. We still must explain why so many of these students who went abroad chose not even to apply to Malaysian universities.

Overseas English medium education was seen as the best channel for advancement, and those who had access to it included the elites of all three communities. (Both Dr. Mahathir and Datuk Musa Hitam had children studying in the United Kingdom).[80] The children of that new Malay middle class upon which the new administration based its support thus followed in the footsteps of the aristocracy. They shared the experience with the children of the non-Malay middle classes who found university places abroad when these were not available to them locally. This university education overseas, and particularly in the English-speaking world, thus served to protect privilege and to create the conditions for economic advancement available to only a small minority.

So far as the non-Malays were concerned, the competition for local places was much more intense than for overseas places (and it is reasonable to infer that the non-Malays accepted into local universities and unable to find the capital to support themselves overseas often represented the brightest and the best of their communities and of their local university generation). For instance, by one calculation the great majority of first-class mathematics degrees awarded by Universiti Malaya went to graduates of Chinese national-type schools. Local standards were perceived by some to be inadequate and declining. A report by students of Universiti Sains Malaysia showed that 66.6 per cent of students considered their lectures and tutorials unsatisfactory.[81] (But students are not always the best judges.)

Many specialisms were still not covered, particularly at post-graduate levels. The few Malays among university staff were concentrated in administration; in 1981 Datuk Musa Hitam, then Minister of Education, admitted "a most serious problem of motivation among Malay academics to go into research and scholarship."[82] Hence most courses were taught in Malay by Chinese lecturers, and sometimes in very bad Malay. A similar contradiction afflicted the supply of textbooks. In 1983 when all universities were to all intents and purposes Malay medium throughout, the library of Universiti Sains Malaysia counted only ten per cent of its book stock, very few of its 35,000 visual aids (and those few mainly religious songs), and none of its 5,000 rolls of micro films in Malay.[83] Other university libraries were no better off. The situation had arisen in part because of the failure of the *Dewan Bahasa dan Pustaka* (Language and Literature Agency, responsible for language planning) to recruit academics to write or translate, despite the generous royalties offered—20 per cent for original texts and up to ten cents a word for translations.[84] (But it must be taken into account that sales were limited. Claiming that it wished to protect the Indonesian printing industry, the Indonesian Government still refused to allow imports of Malaysian textbooks for exhibition or circulation.)[85] One newspaper editorial described the shortage of Malay textbooks as "critical, if not scandalous."[86]

This meant that students who could not read English well enough to cope with English medium textbooks relied for their instruction on the few Malay books available, lectures given in Malay by the predominantly Chinese teaching staff, and lecture hand-outs. Not surprisingly morale dropped among lecturers, many of whom left the profession.[87] And as a result, the exodus of students to study abroad swelled.

The notion of a Malay medium education system had been sold to the electorate on the basis that it would generate a sense of national unity and identity. We have seen the evidence that, so far as a sizeable proportion of the non-Malay communities were concerned, the achievement of that system in 1982-3 failed in this objective. And there was cause for supposing that it had not entirely satisfied the expectations of the Malay community either.

So far as the Malays were concerned, the language and educational legislation was intended to serve three purposes; to safeguard and enhance their political rights, to enable them to compete on at least equal terms with the non-Malays in the economic system, and to develop the use of Malay language for purposes of integrating the nation. It was expected that these three purposes would coincide, and that there would one day be serious business disadvantages in lacking a fluent command of Malay (Carlson 1975, p. 18).

The day indeed came, but paradoxically it ushered in signs that, in the words of the Star headline, the policy had been "too successful." The Deputy Prime Minister, Datuk Musa Hitam, was quoted to the effect that school examinations showed

> the non-Malays were second to none in their use of Bahasa Malaysia.
>
> He said the implications for the Malays were clear—they could no longer afford to take a relaxed view about Bahasa Malaysia just because it was their mother tongue. "The danger is that unless the Malays are willing to accept the realities, they may go back to square one as far as education is concerned," he said.
>
> Datuk Musa said while these were only signs, it was perhaps appropriate for UMNO and its education bureau to start looking into the implementation of the national education policy.[88]

In other words, the non-Malays had made up for the linguistic disadvantages that had been imposed upon them. Indeed, examination results suggested that they were now outstripping the Malays in their own language.[89] They had retained their commercial expertise and their world-wide networks of business partners. The Malays, on the other hand, had not taken full advantage of their opportunities. The Fourth Malaysia Plan revealed that between 1970 and 1980 their mean income had risen only two per cent, from 65 per cent to 67 per cent of the national mean average.[90] The non-Malays were in a strong position to compete with Malays on Malay terms, at least in the economic field. The national language policy had failed to guarantee Malay economic dominance.

We might note in parenthesis that discrimination in favour of the Malays rebounding to their loss had been foreseen twenty-six years earlier. A most prescient Indian delegate to the Federation of Malaya Legislative Council, Mr. K. L. Devaser, had remarked in the debate on the proposals of the Reid Commission in 1957:

> May I with respect and due humility point out that this special position of the Malays has acted to the detriment of the Malays—not the non-Malays. The non-Malays have improved because they are not given a special position.
>
> . . . I think if the Malays had had competition, keen competition, from the other communities, they will be as much forward economically as the other races.[91]

Datuk Musa's statement also demonstrates an important contradiction in the educational and economic policies. When the audience was national, they were expressed in terms of building a common national "Malaysian" identity. Yet when each of the National Front parties addressed its own constituents, it spoke in terms of communal competition. To take an example, on one occasion an MCA leader told his audience of Chinese guild members,

> The Chinese must wake up. There is no time for complacency. We must realise we have duty to fulfil, to ourselves, to the generations that come after us and to the nation we call ours.
>
> . . . The Chinese have been complacent compared with the dynamic thrusts of Malays and Malay organisations into commerce and industry. The Malays are today forging ahead with good results. What happened to the proud Chinese? What happened to Chinese dominance in mining, banking and finance?[92]

In a second example, less than two years before one MCA minister was brushing aside complaints that the Government should take greater responsibility for administering the POL programmes in schools (as we have seen), a second had urged a meeting of 250 Chinese associations that all Chinese should learn Mandarin in the interests of communal solidarity and economic development.[93]

So although the leading members of the Government parties may have enjoyed a commonality of interest, they were sometimes obliged to respond to the fact that their electorates viewed society in terms of communal competition. This supports those critics on the left who argue that the elites played upon communal loyalties and fears in order to whip their masses into line, and thus preserve the Alliance system and disguise the class realities.

In this chapter we set out to demonstrate why the Government chose not to implement language policy in the legal system before 1981. The policy was sold to the electorate on the basis that it would be applied throughout public life and create a common denominator between the communities. It was implemented first in the new education system because this seemed to offer the greatest political rewards in terms of honouring this commitment to national unity. How far the elites of the Alliance parties were actually concerned to encourage communal brotherhood and to break down the barricades is left open to conjecture. In any event, the successful administration of the language/education policy by 1982 failed to usher in the promised unity.

Why, in 1981 and twenty-four years after Independence, did the new administration decide then to spread the language policy to the legal system? Three reasons have been given. First, the prime minister did not enjoy the royal connections and English-medium legal education shared by his predecessors; he based his political power on the support of a new Malay middle class just as untouched as he was by commitment to the old institutions. He could afford to introduce language reforms in the legal system with relative impunity. A demonstration by lawyers, both Malay and non-Malay, against amendments to the Societies Act in April 1981 received little public interest and was easily brushed aside. The profession showed little capability to harness extra-parliamentary political emotions.

Second, the policy symbolized Malay dominance, and the continuation gave the new administration legitimacy among the Malay community. The Government was within sight of fulfilling the historical obligation to apply it within the education system (although Datuk Musa had suggested that some areas of education demanded further attention). The legal system offered an opportunity to continue the policy and to discharge the promise that Malay should be the language used throughout public life.

Third, the affects of implementation had thus far disappointed both Malays and non-Malays, and had generated further dissatisfaction. The notion that national unity and economic justice would automatically predicate the creation of a Malay-medium education system had proved a chimera. The UMNO elite needed to extend the policy in order to protect themselves against Malay bitterness; for as long as the policy was not fully implemented throughout society, the Government could argue that it could not be fairly judged. The opposition of the non-Malays merited far less attention. They were represented in the Alliance by parties that, since 1969, had accepted a Malay definition of national unity, and were content to restrict their political initiatives to distributing patronage and making appeals for the cultural integrity of their communities. The almost total lack of comment by the MCA and MIC on the implementation of the national language policy within the legal system suggested that the UMNO elite had read the situation correctly and had succeeded in imposing their limitations on political debate.

CHAPTER THREE

The Legal System

Chapter 2 showed that the 1967 National Language Act was intended to answer Malay demands that the commitment to the national language policy be honoured. Parliament returned a vote of 95 to 11 (these mostly PMIP members), and the Act was generally welcomed. Given these circumstances, the anomolous status granted to the law may be interpreted as a legitimate expression of public will. Clause 8 secured the continued use of English:

> All proceedings (other than the giving of evidence by a witness) in the Federal Court, the High Court or any subsidiary court shall be in the national language or in the English language or partly in the national language and partly in the English language.
>
> Provided that the Court may, either of its own motion or on the application of any party to the proceedings and after considering the interests of justice in those proceedings, order that the proceedings (other than the giving of evidence by a witness) shall be wholly in the national language or wholly in the English language.[1]

This clause absolved the courts from having to use Malay, and for reasons that we shall see, most took advantage of it. Some cases were heard in the national language before the October 1981 Directive requiring the use of Malay was issued; by one count Malay was used in 2,500 cases between 1976 and mid-1981, [2] and in October 1980 the Federal Court had heard its first criminal appeal in Malay.[3] But the Directive marked the turning point, and it had an immediate affect. Butterworth Magistrates' Courts began using Malay within a fortnight,[4] and Kuala Lumpur Courts for all mention hearings a fortnight after that.[5] In November the High Court in Alor Star for the first time used Malay throughout a criminal case,[6] and a month later the High Court in Johore Baru became the first in the country to employ the language throughout a civil case relating to a land issue.[7] By January 1983, ninety per cent of all lower court cases in Pahang were being conducted in Malay.[8]

The newspaper reports of progress in using legal Malay need to be taken with reservation. My own observations and comments made by lawyers suggest that the figure claimed for Pahang was far from typical. On the west coast, where the non-Malay communities are most dense, the figure seemed to be around fifty per cent. The Lord President Tun Mohamed Suffian Hashim commented that

Malay had been adopted "not much in Kuala Lumpur. But in other towns . . . fairly extensively."[9]

The rate of change was certainly too slow in the eyes of some critics. One judge described progress as "extremely discouraging," and not in keeping with progress in other areas of life.[10] This impatience was justified by one reading of the Directive that courts were obliged to use Malay, but as noted on page 1, the Directive left a loophole. Those courts that delayed found justification in the final provision and in a follow-up circular issued by the Chief Registrar's Deputy on 12 October 1981. The use of Malay was not absolutely compulsory. Courts were instructed to take into account "the complexity of the case in question, counsels' mastery of Malay and the possibility of the hearing being postponed if Malay was employed."[11] The choice of language was left largely to the discretion of the bench. The courts should continue to regard the administration of justice as their primary objective, and where one party's lack of proficiency in Malay was so great that it was unable to properly present its case and where this would affect the verdict, then English should be used.

Previous chapters looked at those features of the political environment that explained the delay in implementing the language policy in the legal system, and then the decision to issue the Directive. It was shown how the move to formulate a national culture policy was influenced by political considerations. This chapter answers the same two questions (Why not before 1981? Why then?) by first discussing the conditions allowed by the follow-up circular to justify instances in which Malay was not employed as the language of the court (the complexity of the case, counsel's mastery of Malay, and the possibility of postponements arising from the use of Malay). These direct our attention to those features of the court system that militated against change. They reveal the administration's analysis of why it could not yet enforce the compulsory use of Malay, and hence, its analysis of what was wrong with the implementation of the existing system of laws. The first half of the chapter asks how far this analysis was correct. The second half demonstrates how far pressures for reform went beyond correcting these apparent abuses, and considers the influences of calls for a national culture.

The complexity of a case in court was determined in practice by the need to argue from a body of law and the medium of this literature. Where the law had been translated or needed only cursory reference, implementing the language policy presented few problems. Where circumstances demanded debate of statutes and judgements published only in English, the court was swayed to employ English. When the Directive was issued, the mass of law was English-medium only.

The Government recognised the practical difficulties of working without Malay language texts. In June 1981—that is, four months before the Directive was issued—it stipulated that Malay would be made compulsory only when all necessary translations had been made.[12] The lack of legal terminology and of a body of law in Malay had carried some of the blame for the failure of the very brief attempt to implement language policy in the courts in 1970 during the period of reassessment that followed the 1969 communal riots. (The backlog of cases had also been held responsible, and we shall look at the continuing effects of postponements below.) A year after the Directive was issued, only sixty laws passed before 1967 had been translated. These were the most frequently cited—for instance, the Penal Code, Criminal Procedure Code, Road Traffic Ordinance. A further ten laws, including the Malay version of the Constitution, were still waiting to be gazetted.[13] Furthermore, any incentive to employ the Malay version or to agitate for more translations was weakened by the practice of first drafting bills in English and then translating them and marking the English versions definitive.[14] Federal Court judgements began to be systematically translated only when the Judiciary Department set up its own bureau with this responsibility in early 1983.[15] But a body of literature is not the only means by which the lawyer informed himself about the law, and perhaps not even the most important. Twining and Uglow (1981) suggest that

> It is wrong to assume in any jurisdiction, especially a small one, that writing is the main medium of communication about law. The telephone, formal lectures, informal lunches and even social occasions all feature frequently in most jurisdictions as channels for oral communication about law and, it seems, most professionals rely as much on oral as written sources for obtaining and updating the information they need.[16]

This point was not raised. Although some lawyers argued that the switch should be made compulsory only when all lawyers and court officials had mastered spoken courtroom Malay[17] (as opposed to written Malay), no one specified that it be delayed until they had mastered the informal spoken registers. That day was a long way off, and Chinese and Indian professionals were still far more likely to use their own languages or English out of court and on social occasions. So insofar as the language of non-courtroom activities continued to be the "main medium of communication about law" the legal system would be practised in two media; the medium *of* the law (increasingly Malay) and the medium *about* the law (other languages). Hence the implementation of a culture and language policy designed to create national unity was likely to lead to the development of a bilingual profession—divided not by community, but by professional function.

In parenthesis, the absence of translations was apparently more damaging in the medical profession. In 1980, doctors complained that of the seventeen titles that had been translated, only six had been published and the remaining eleven were either unsatisfactory or had been overtaken by new editions of the originals.[18] This meant that almost all medical teaching had to be in English.[19] Lawyers were not penalized to this extent.

In summary, the paucity of a Malay medium literature partially explained why language policy had not been implemented in the legal system before 1981, and why some objections were raised when the Directive was issued. But it was not decisive, and in the event the court system continued to operate, things went on much as before.

The significance of counsels' mastery of Malay (the second mitigating factor allowed by the follow-up circular) is dealt with here in terms of the profession's communal composition, and the extent to which Malay and non-Malay lawyers' attitudes towards implementing the use of Malay were determined by communal loyalties and mother-tongue competence in the language. How far courtroom proceedings influenced the court's use of Malay or English is examined more thoroughly in the next chapter.

In 1981 the great majority of courtroom lawyers were not Malay by ethnic origin, and did not have Malay as their mother tongue; 1,110 of the 1,296 on the rolls of the Bar Council were non-Malay.[20] Nevertheless, this essentially non-Malay profession served all communal and social groups and enjoyed high status. In these respects it stood on its own. The leadership of the trade unions was predominantly non-Malay and Indian,[21] but was of low status. The officer corps in the armed forces and police were recruited mostly from the Malays. The political parties (including such opposition parties as the DAP, supposedly non-communal but in reality predominantly Chinese) and all newspapers save the small English language press read only by the upper- and middle-class minority, served communal aspirations. Hence the Bar, and the legal system that it served, demonstrated the non-Malays making an important contribution to society.

But although the Bar was overwhelmingly non-Malay, a majority of Federal judges and an increasing number of presidents of Sessions Courts and magistrates were Malay. The Government legal service was appointing Malays and non-Malays in the proportion of seven to two. This was made feasible by the growth of the Faculty of Law established in the Universiti Malaya in 1972 with the specific objective of training Malays for the Government service. (Unlike in England, in Malaysia and in general, first class magistrates have at least first degrees in law.) By 1980 the Faculty had admitted 391 Malay students.[22] The syllabus was based on that taught in England and Singapore, but also dealt with Muslim and Malaysian Native Customary Law.[23] This local specialisation was almost entirely irrelevant to the existing civil legal system as practised in Magistrates' and all higher courts, but it laid the groundwork for a revised legal system incorporating indigenous law. It also trained Malay lawyers to appear in Penghulu and Shariah courts, although admittedly, the financial rewards were insufficient to tempt more than a dedicated handful, who also needed to be qualified religious teachers.[24] The demand for lawyers and the difficulty in satisfying this demand led Universiti Sains Malaysia to plan a similar four-year law degree course to begin in 1984.[25]

All law graduates who had studied on Government grants were bonded to the Government legal service for up to ten years. A majority of the men were likely to serve at least some of those ten years in the magistracy. (In part because the regulation that a magistrate should not serve for more than two years in any one court seemed to place women at a greater inconvenience, no women were employed in the magistracy after 1979; most went into the drafting service.) Many Malays seemed quite happy with this arrangement. The office of magistrate brought them high regard within their communities. However, at least as many looked for every opportunity to buy themselves out from their bonds and to leave the legal service— not to enroll at the Bar, but to join industry. Because companies above a certain size were obliged to employ Malays on the quota of a least 30 per cent at all levels of the organization, they were prepared to pay extremely generous salaries to Malay executives, and in particular to the few Malay corporation lawyers. This enforced demand for scarce executive talent encouraged companies to offer increasingly unrealistic salaries. This led to considerable job-hopping among the available supply of qualified Malays, and many companies were seriously effected by a high-turnover of senior Malay staff and the subsequent discontinuity. The Government increased the penalties imposed on Malay scholarship law students who broke bond in an attempt to ensure that they were not lost to the legal service.

Their different communal memberships might suggest that Bar and bench held opposing attitudes toward the implementation of the language policy and reform of the legal system. But communal factors counted for less than training. Despite the introduction of legal education in Malaysian institutions, the great majority of the profession had studied law in English-medium universities abroad. In 1981, about a thousand Malaysians were studying law at undergraduate level in Britain alone,[26] a further 210 (including Singaporeans) were reading for their Bar finals in the Inns of Court,[27] and many more were studying in Australia, New Zealand, Singapore, and India. It was understandable that many of those who returned home would prefer to practice the system of law that they had studied (English or essentially English) in the language in which they had studied it. This applied equally to Malays and non-Malays. By 1981 probably only fifty-five Malay members of the legal profession had trained throughout in the medium of Malay.[28]

The commitment that both Malay and non-Malay lawyers made to the English legal system in which they had trained was determined by professional loyalties. In common they enjoyed a high status that raised them above communal antagonisms. They constituted an elite, but an elite determined by professional qualifications rather than by blood like the traditional Malay rulers, or commercial success like the Chinese leaders. Their dedication to legal traditions and the ideal of justice was exemplified by the reaction of Mr. Karpal Singh, a DAP

Member of Parliament and lawyer, to a 1980 suggestion that Malay replace English.

> Even prominent judges have expressed their views that English should be the medium of the courts. Our laws are based on English laws. It would be virtually impossible to translate English law books and reports into Bahasa. We must be practical and pragmatic. It is not being anti-national to say that at the moment English law is here to stay, unless we can evolve a legal system which is practical and acceptable to the people. Even then, it would have its roots in the English law, the oldest legal system in the world.[29]

Mr. Singh had a political axe to grind, and his argument echoed the stock DAP policy that a legitimate national culture—in this case a national legal culture—could not be imposed but must evolve. But the relationship he found between the language of the cultural practice and the practice itself made a philosophical point. In effect he stated the "strong" sociolinguistic position (see for instance Whorf 1962, Mandelbaum's 1966 collection of essays on Sapir, and the summary in Bell 1976, pp. 29-30, 63) that language does not merely reflect the essence of social activity but determines it. The proposal to translate English law not only threatened the profession's traditions, but the use of Malay would foster the development of Malay legal concepts, and over time generate a hybrid legal system. This was to be feared not only because it would enforce elements of Malay culture on Malays and non-Malays alike, but because it threatened to undermine the traditions bred by allegiance to "the oldest legal system in the world."

The third condition under which courts might continue to use English was the possibility of a hearing being postponed if Malay were used. This factor had been used by the Government to explain the failure of the previous attempt to implement the language policy in 1970. But a case might have to be postponed for a range of other reasons, and it is argued here that although the court's choice of language might slow proceedings, it was not the most significant cause.

Accused persons or witnesses quite often failed to appear.[30] The accused might fail to pay his counsel before the hearing or fail to reach agreement on how he should be represented.[31] One lawyer complained

> There were some instances recently when some fellas whom I don't know at all told the magistrates that P. G. Segran is their lawyer. I didn't have a clue about them until some P. O. (prosecuting officer) passes by and says: "Segran, quick! The court is waiting for you."
>
> I went to the court, I saw the joker, a complete stranger whom I scolded for using my name and informed the court I was not acting for him. The magistrate rebuked him for misleading the court.[32]

Postponements were also forced on the court by the increasing tendency of unrepresented accused to apply for legal aid and representation when a trial was already underway. (One investigating officer blamed this new awareness of legal rights and unwillingness to plead guilty on Malaysian television broadcasting too many American crime series.) The following example illustrates the frustration this could cause the court. In the second hearing, one of the accused has just applied for representation.

(A)
Magistrate: When was this case registered? In nineteen, July nineteen eighty.
Accused: I never realised it would come to this your honour that we would have to defend ourselves.
Magistrate: You never realised you would have to defend yourselves?
Accused: That it would come to this situation.
Magistrate: What situation? That you would stand inside the dock?
Accused: Yes your honour.

(Kuala Kuba Baru Magistrate's Court: 20.3.1981)

This example shows that postponements were caused because the laymen either did not understand the court system, or exploited the laxity with which it was enforced. But counsel might be equally responsible for delay. A second lawyer explained the tendency to take on too much work and double-book appearances in different courts:

> Some lawyers take more than they can swallow. They take up the cases then pass it on to the junior lawyers in the firm which I think is bad.[33]

An example is given of one case involving the theft of jewelry worth a total of Malaysian $1,300, postponed for the eleventh time.

> The case was first mentioned on November 29, 1979. It was mentioned another four times before the first hearing on Jan. 29 last year.
>
> After that, 10 different hearing dates were postponed.
>
> The case was last heard on Jan. 5 this year.
>
> Counsel for Thevendiran, Mr. M. S. Dhillon, applied for postponement today because he said he was engaged at the Kuala Lumpur Sessions Court. . . . The magistrate granted a final postponement after counsel for the second accused, Mr. K. Pasupathy, had assured him that he would appear for both accused should Mr. Dhillon be engaged elsewhere on Oct. 4.[34]

Lawyers tended to excuse this practice by pointing to the likelihood of postponement arising from other causes. If they never double-booked appearances, they would waste considerable time in waiting, and lose employment. Hence delay led to further delay and the spiral tightened.

Court procedure might make matters worse. In the lower courts all cases were prosecuted by police inspectors who usually only received their briefs on the morning of the hearing. Witnesses had been called by the investigating officers, and if the prosecuting officer decided to examine a witness who had not been listed, he too was obliged to ask for a postponement. These problems were exacerbated by the shortage of court officials at all levels.[35] In 1982 the population of 14.5 million was served by only thirty-four judges.[36] (These figures might be compared to Trinidad's population of 1.4 million and 17 judges.) The same year there were only 94 Magistrates' Courts in the country.[37] Each court was served by one first-class magistrate, who also acted as registrar. The magistrate sitting in Petaling Jaya, Selangor State, served a population of 60,000 and had a jurisdiction over civil cases in which a claim was being made for up to Malaysian $10,000 and criminal cases in which the maximum sentence for the offense was fourteen years in prison—very similar to the jurisdiction of an English County Court. We have already noted the financial incentives offered to Malay lawyers by private industry and the quota system operated in respect of Malays and non-Malays by the Government legal service. These two factors meant that where Malays could not be recruited, vacancies went unfilled.

In summary, too few courts, too few court officials, and too few lawyers were trying to handle a growing workload. The following figures from the High Court of Pahang, at Kuantan demonstrate how difficult it was to dispose of an increasing number of cases.[38]

	cases heard	disposed of	postponed
1981	399	183	216
1982	504	239	265

In the same years Kuantan was served by only one magistrate rather than the stipulated two.

Problems arising from the accused person or witness wishing to give evidence in some language other than Malay were overcome by the use of interpreters. The use of interpreters started in colonial times and, by 1981, a Magistrates' Court had a complement of at least four able to interpret between English and Malay, Tamil, Punjabi, and Mandarin, and access to supernumerary staff if, for instance, a witness spoke one of the less common Chinese dialects. When the witness and accused spoke different languages and neither spoke the language of the court, two interpreters were used, one to interpret the evidence to the court and the second to interpret it to the accused. A number of procedural difficulties arose which are discussed in the next chapter. However, because interpreters were always available (at least for the more important languages), the use of languages of other than Malay was not the most important cause of postponements.

We have seen how far the mitigating factors permitted by the follow-up circular to the Directive represented a correct analysis of the reasons why the use of Malay could not be made compulsory, and explained the delay in imposing language policy. We have seen that although significant, they were not decisive in preventing the use of Malay. We now consider why the move to switch to Malay in the legal system received support.

Support came from different groups for a range of reasons. There were those who interpreted policy narrowly as the simple substitution of Malay for English, and hoped that this would encourage the growth of national unity. This aspect of language policy has been dealt with in the previous chapters. There were those who saw it as one means of reforming a legal system that was showing signs of strain, and those who interpreted policy most broadly as the first step towards the development of an indigenous legal system based on the national culture. We are concerned here with these two latter groups. They were influenced to varying degrees by the internal problems that the system faced in administering justice, the difficulties experienced by the layman, the degree of dependence on the English system, and a desire to develop an indigenous system. The extent to which the reformers identified the implementation of language policy with more sweeping changes in the legal system is exemplified by the October 1980 editorial in the newsletter of the Penang Bar Committee, *Suara Peguam*. The newsletter commented that

> due to the doctrine of binding (or is it blinding) precedent and the British precedents of 99% of our laws it is not possible to implement Bahasa Malaysia in our courts; for what British judges decide today in English courts is followed here the next day . . . . Unless the powers that be are prepared to abolish their doctrine of blind obedience to British laws and replace it with a Malaysian based legal system, it is not possible to implement Bahasa Malaysia.

Mr. Karpal Singh's fears that the switch to Malay would lead inexorably to a Malay system, discussed above, were made in response. They expressed the other side of the same coin.

The internal problems that the system faced in administering justice are dealt with first. The extent to which efficiency was compromised by postponements and the causes of postponements have been noted. We go on to look at the evidence that the layman was often unable to cope with the most basic points of legal administration. The fragment of courtroom data quoted in example (A) above showed that the accused apparently did not realise that a charge would lead to an appearance in court. According to one lawyer, eighty per cent of his clients did not know what they were being charged with.[39] Gurdial Singh Nijar (1978) showed that of his sample of approximately forty unrepresented accused who pleaded not guilty in Kuala Lumpur Magistrates' courts in 1973, 100 per cent failed to make a submission at the end of either the prosecution case or the defence case, 34 per cent failed to cross-examine at all (and the cross-examinations conducted by the other 66 per cent consisted of little more than protestations of innocence); and not surprisingly, all but one were found guilty. An example of the cross-examination made by an unrepresented accused is given below. The witness claims that he assaulted her.

(B) Magistrate: You understand what she said? You've got any questions to ask? (INTERPRETER/ACCUSED: CHINESE INTERACTION)
Interpreter: He says he tried to talk to you. Is it true?
Magistrate: Is it true?
Witness: No he didn't say a single word all. He tried to hold my hand. (INTERPRETER/ACCUSED: CHINESE INTERACTION)
Witness: He tried to catch my hands.
Magistrate: He tried to catch my hands. Yes next question. (INTERPRETER/ACCUSED: CHINESE INTERACTION)
Interpreter: I didn't at any time grab her hands.
Witness: Yes.
Magistrate: He said he did not grab your hands. Is that true?
Witness: No he tried to grab my hands.

(Kuala Lumpur Magistrates' Courts: 12 January 1982)

Rather than substantiate his innocence, the accused simply provides the witness with additional opportunities to register her complaint.

In a further paper (1982) dealing with the access of the common man to legal institutions and processes, Gurdial Singh Nijar made the important point that

> our legal system is based on self-identification of jury and wrong and self-selection of a remedy. Amongst the poor, as we have seen, this self-identification process is virtually non-operative. Consequently the viability of the legal system, in relation to poverty communities (sic) at least, is questionable. (p. 5)

The poor and uneducated in any society are least likely to exploit the legal remedies available, and this is not merely the case where the legal system owes more to foreign than to indigenous influences. Gurdial Singh Nijar's frequent references (in 1978, and a further paper on the same theme, 1981) to Carlen's study of very similar abuses suffered in London Magistrates' Courts (1976), make the point well. In an ideal world, a government would engage in economic and educational programmes that raised the lease privileged law "consumer" to the level at which he was sufficiently educated, wealthy, and self-confident to obtain value for money from the legal system. In practice, the problem is invariably defined in socio-legal rather than socio-economic terms, and the legal system is expected to provide the palliative.

Previous generations of Malayans have tried to avoid entanglement in the colonial legal system. The layman of every community had found it more convenient to plead guilty or to settle out of court. Interpreters had served to mediate in disputes between members of different communities or between the accused and the court. The next chapter provides examples of the interpreter still carrying out this traditional function. The legal system did not impinge on the layman's life to the extent that the education system did, and hence calls for reform, including implementation of the language policy, did not generate the same degree of emotion. But there was general disquiet, expressed on a popular level by the campaign waged by the *New Straits Times* against malpractice in 1982. Despite some complaints by some lawyers of prejudice, the campaign struck a nerve.

The reformers included academic lawyers (for instance Koh 1982) who were not primarily interested in the full application of the national culture. Even the more conservative members of the profession agree that the legal system needed overhauling. In an interview, Tun Mohamed Suffian noted the existence of a Commission for Law Revision and added that

> revising the law is important but not as important as law reform. We also need a Law Reform Commission or Committee.[40]

This proposal was welcomed by the Bar Council.[41] And there were other straws in the wind. In October 1982, the Government presented the Penal Code and Criminal Procedure Code (Amendment) Bill to Parliament with the purposes of ensuring "public order and religious freedom."[42] The Bar Council set up a Legal Aid Centre available to those with a monthly income not exceeding Malaysian $591 and disposable assets not exceeding Malaysian $3,500. The Centre provided services in the areas of family law, industrial accidents, employment, tenancy matters, detentions under three main acts, consumer problems, and criminal cases.[43] It was designed to complement the Government's Legal Aid Bureau, which restricted its services to persons with a monthly income of only Malaysian $62.50 and assets of less than Malaysian $500. In March 1983 the Government announced plans to organise one-year courses leading up to a locally administered Bar examination from 1985. This move was intended to resolve the difficulties that had arisen when the London Senate of Inns and Council of Legal Education had raised the requirements for entry to courses leading to London Bar examinations. It would have the secondary function of training law graduates specifically for practice in local courts.[44]

The organisation of local bar examinations gave only one indication of the desire to rid the Malaysian system of dependence on the English system. This tendency was by no means new. In January 1978 appeals to the Privy Council on criminal and constitutional issues had been stopped. After Dr. Mahathir's administration came to power, the pressure increased for abolition in civil cases also. In October 1981 a Deputy Minister in the Prime Minister's Department, Datuk Abdullah Rahman, announced in Parliament that the Government "felt that judges in the country had now reached a high professional standard" and it was "seriously considering" abolishing the appeal system.[45] A *New Straits Times* editorial gave its support:

> In a large proportion of appeals from Malaysia to the UK, the Privy Council affirms the decision of the Federal Court. For the years 1957 - 1977, the percentage of decisions upheld was 90 per cent in criminal cases and 71 per cent in civil litigation.
>
> There is also the persuasive argument that laws must be understood in the context of the prevailing economic, social, and security conditions . . . . A judge can fulfill his functions adequately only if he has knowledge of the social facts surrounding the law and the social effects on society of his judicial precepts. It is time that final judgements in Malaysian cases come from judges who have to live with the social costs of their judgements.[46]

In other words, a Malaysian legal system should reflect the society's values. In January of the following year the same Deputy Minister announced that the Government had "no plans" to either stop appeals or to set up a Supreme Court.[47] But in October, plans to abolish the system were announced, this time by another Deputy Minister in the Prime Minister's Department. The press report added that

> there were, however, no plans to set up a Supreme Court to replace the Council.[48]

Two months later, the current Lord President, Tun Mohamed Suffian, informed the editorial board of the Bar Council's quarterly journal *Insaf* (reported in the January edition) that the Government had agreed in principle to set up a Supreme Court to hear appeals. The delay in setting up this court was "possibly because of the lack of accommodations."[49]

It should be noted that this crab-like shift to espousal of a Supreme Court to replace the Privy Council passed with very little comment, and this is instructive. The administration's problems in commanding a consensus within the Malay community and the Alliance parties meant that controversial proposals for policy were presented only gradually and with considerable equivocation. The administration appeared to adopt a strong stand on issues that could be represented as vital to national integrity and were of no very serious cost to any one community—for instance, the furor over fees charged by British universities. But on issues that were of immediate domestic interest, it played a more pragmatic game. For instance, the decision to implement language policy in the courts, the abolition of appeals to the Privy Council, the "3Rs" policy (insofar as the critics were correct and this really did conceal an attempt to bring the national-type schools into the national system), the proposed obligatory courses in Islamic studies for university undergraduates—in all these cases statements were made and then contradicted. In the face of real opposition, the original proposals were dropped or modified or qualified. Where a policy was discovered to be uncontroversial (as in the first two examples) it was pushed further. Only a few objections were raised to the abolition of appeal to the Privy Council.

We have discussed the difficulties faced by the layman who perhaps neither understood the system nor the language in which it was practised, and have noticed the measures of reform supported by the legal profession. Some critics went further in diagnosing the ills of the system and suggesting remedies which would precipitate the development of a new, indigenous system. For instance, the President of the Consumers' Association of Penang, Encik S. M. Mohamed Idris, argued in his opening address to the 1982 Seminar that

> Our present laws and legal system have been handed down as a colonial legacy. There is thus a strong bias towards confrontation rather than conciliation, as is found in Eastern traditional culture. Perhaps greater research should be directed to the development of the law of the indigenous, local context. Perhaps our law researchers should look back into our history and culture and rediscover a legal system that will have more relevance to the Malaysian situation. (pp. 2-3)

There had never been a single indigenous legal system. Indeed, Hooker (1978) shows that legal pluralism was a common characteristic of all Southeast Asian systems. Elsewhere (Hooker, 1972) he describes how Shariah law and the customary land tenure law of *adat* had developed side by side with little conflict, mainly because they dealt with different areas of life. *Adat* had once ruled on serious criminal offences, but these now belonged within the jurisdiction of the civil system. *Adat* varied widely in different states. For instance, descent in Negri Sembilan, parts of Malacca, and one or two areas in Perak and Johore was matrilineal, elsewhere patrilineal. He demonstrates the bewildering range of rules governing inter- and intra-clan marriage in one state alone (Negri Sembilan). Neither *adat* nor Shariah deal with contract or tort, and to all intents and purposes, neither system affected non-Muslims.

The notion of Eastern traditional culture as conciliatory may have been equally fanciful. However, a usable cultural past need not have historical veracity. That it represents an ideal, now lost but still recoverable, is sufficient. The myth of a golden age worked as powerfully in the new atmosphere of nationalism as did the image of the alienated layman adrift in a colonial legal system that he failed to understand. Moreover Encik Mohamed's argument agreed with official policy.

The administration supported the cause of reform, but looked for changes a good deal more radical than those countenanced by practising lawyers. Indeed, statements made by UMNO politicians paid little attention to the problems that worried the profession. They wanted change for other reasons. In their eyes, policies to enforce the use of the national language, to end dependence on colonial institutions, and to reform the legal system were interrelated and belonged under the umbrella of the national culture policy. The younger UMNO leaders most sympathetic to Dr. Mahathir's particular brand of nationalism belonged to and drew their support from the burgeoning Malay middle class (see Lev 1979, p. 41). This new urban middle class aspired to establish its identity against the Chinese middle class, and the concept of Malaysian society based by law on Malay cultural values seemed to satisfy this need. An UMNO MP speaking in the lower house made the administration's priorities clear.

> In introducing a motion of thanks to the Yang di-Pertuan Agong for his opening address yesterday, Haji Shamsuri referred to the "lack of interest" in fully using Bahasa Malaysia by the judiciary. He said such a state of affairs was a pity since the country has been independent for 25 years. He then cited the attire of judges at yesterday's opening as a clear example of the "left-over from the colonial day." He said only two wore *songkoks* [Malay hats]. The rest wore wigs.[50]

The association made between the use of Malay, national identity, and costume was significant. Costume, like all artefacts, was valued for its function as a social symbol; the *songkok* was an element of Malay dress not normally worn by non-Malays, and its use should demonstrate the Malay base of the national culture and the legal system. The objection to the judicial wig was not as "trivial" as some writers suggest (Zakaria Haji Ahmad 1982, p. 90).

The same equation had been formulated a few months earlier in even wider terms.

> Several Senators have urged the Government to fully implement the use of Bahasa Malaysia in the courts. . . . The Senators made these remarks when debating the Courts of Judicature (Amendment) Bill in the Dewan Negara today. . . . Senator Ibrahim Abdullah said the use of the English language in the courts should be abolished because most of the people in the country were more proficient in Bahasa Malaysia.
>
> The question of the terminology used in the courts should not arise at all as the Dewan Bahasa dan Pustaka had already prepared the necessary terminology. Senator Ibrahim also suggested that the present laws be based on the Islamic laws. He added that judges should be sent to Pakistan to study and assess how Islamic laws were being practised in the country. He also urged the Government to stop the present practice of allowing appeals for civil cases to be heard before the Privy Council in London as it would affect the integrity of the country's legal officers. Senator Hajjah Salmah Sheikh Hussain, in supporting the Bill, hoped that the attire for judges be changed to suit the national culture.[51]

The Malay champions of an enforced national culture perceived artefacts as symbols of cultural identity, and in their eyes the judges' preference for the apparel legitimated by the traditions to which they had been educated indicated at least apathy, if not resistance. The judges, and most lawyers whether Malay or non-Malay, might have preferred to distinguish between national cultural and legal cultural loyalties. In the absence of a single articulated indigenous legal system they were obliged to administer the system as it stood and as expediently as possible. The proposal that judges be sent for training in Pakistan reflected an increasingly intransigent interpretation given to the need for an indigenous legal system. Indonesia offered a model of a system that represented ethnic Malay values, but this was still heavily influenced by Dutch law. The Pakistani system could claim affinity only insofar as it was based on Islam, but this was apparently sufficient. Hence the first principle of the First National Culture Congress —that the national culture should be based on the indigenous culture of the region—was interpreted in terms of the third—that Islam should be an important element of the national culture. It had become the determining element. The second principle—that features of non-Malay cultures should be incorporated into the national culture if they were not antagonistic to Malay culture—was more honoured in the breach. The assurance given that the Morals Law would also "include the philosophy, tenents and theology of other religions[52] seemed to mean that the teachings of other religions would be acknowledged to the extent that they corresponded with Islam. A normative concept of a national culture inspired by the religion of the Malays found no room for the secular aspects of these cultures.

A final example demonstrates the administration's desire for a more fundamental reform than merely switching languages. The *Star* reported that Dr. Mahathir

> does not rule out the possibility of Malaysia adopting an Islamic rule and assures the people not to be worried over this.
>
> "We have been extremely reasonable in this country. We have not tried to force the non-Muslims to accept anything that is against their conscience," he said.
>
> "We don't want to impose our will. That is not the proper thing to do but there may be a time when everybody accepts Islam and then, of course, at that time there would be no problem."

This suggests that the administration preferred that all communities come to accept Islam of their free will, and when that day arrived, an Islamic system of law would be introduced. But if the communities failed to reach this common ground, the administration might feel obliged to enforce Islamic law without the option. The evidence that we have reviewed suggests that the non-Malays were increasingly unlikely to welcome this situation; that the nature of the Malaysian political system militated against such a consensus; and that Dr. Mahathir's pronouncement was intended not only for the non-Malays but also for those Malays who doubted the administration's commitment to Malay culture.

This chapter first examined those factors that were perceived to hinder the full implementation of the language policy in the legal system, and then considered proposals for changing the system. Lawyers, both Malay and non-Malay, were bound by professional and educational ties that cut across communal boundaries. This common interest in maintaining tradition and the lack of a body of Malay language law had prevented previous implementation of the national language. By 1981 the courts were under considerable pressure, which was demonstrated by the causes for which hearings might be postponed. But no reason can be discerned for supposing that a switch to a Malay medium system would necessarily speed court business, even though a far larger proportion of the population now had some knowledge of Malay than when a brief attempt was made to apply language policy after the 1969 riots.

The profession showed signs of accepting some measure of reform, but was not convinced of the need to accept radical demands that the implementation of language policy should constitute the first step in implementing culture policy. In the main, lawyers wished to limit change to procedural as opposed to substantive issues. Professional interests tended to override communal interests, and this suggested the development of a professional middle class which was not divided along communal lines.

The implementation of the language policy in the legal system provided further evidence of the administration's determination to replace lingering British influences with Malaysian values. The majority of the population was not directly touched— most people in any community manage to keep clear of the courts— just as the furor over the fees charged by British universities was of immediate interest to only a small minority. But this did not detract from the worth of the issue to the administration. It deflected PAS's accusations of neglecting the poor Malays and Malay culture. It appealed to the masses of all communities, who were more likely than the middle classes to face criminal charges and suffer the inconveniences of an overburdened court system, and less likely to speak fluent English and hence to question the value of the switch to Malay. It diverted attention from the disappointments that had accompanied the conversion to a Malay medium education system, and it fulfilled a long established commitment.

CHAPTER FOUR

Language Policy in the Courts

Thus far we have seen how the implementation of language policy in the legal system was influenced by outside factors—by political forces and cultural policies, the development of language policy in the education system, and the composition of the legal profession. In this chapter we see how the lawyer's use of language to perform his professional duties affected the implementation of justice, and to what extent his decision to use Malay or English was determined by courtroom procedure. He needed to apply sophisticated forensic skills, and if he had been trained in English, he often preferred to use it. We then look at how the process of interpreting between witness and court obstructed the strict implementation of procedure. We conclude by noting counsel's problems in employing Malay legal terminology. Much of this chapter involves detailed consideration of the nature of legal language. Sociolinguistic description of legal data demonstrates the difficulties that afflicted the court system, and more generally, suggests how analysis of extended spoken discourse can be applied to explaining sociological phenomena. The description here is non-formal. (For the literature on discourse analysis see Coulthard 1977 and Stubbs 1983; for a formal analysis, Sinclair and Coulthard 1975.)

It was one thing for policy-makers to dictate those fields in which Malay should be used and to specify the appropriate terminology and grammatical structures. It was quite another to enforce rules of language use on the individual. The professional's attitude towards the language policy depended on a number of factors that included his audience and accountability to them, and the nature of his professional activity.

The teacher and politician play significant public roles. We saw in chapter 2 that the teacher had very little option but to use Malay in his classroom duties. The politician was similarly constrained when addressing an audience. A few examples from the data demonstrate the point. DAP members who used English in Parliament were seen to be making a political point and were censored, despite their pleas that they had not yet had a chance to learn Malay.[1] Prime Minister Datuk Hussein Onn was obliged to explain to Parliament

> that he spoke in English at the recent Gerakan general assembly because he wanted to make sure that his speech was understood by everybody.[2]

That even a respected Prime Minister was not immune to criticisms from his usually loyal supporters if he should depart from accepted language practice showed the symbolic importance of the issue. The reason he gave jarred with the radical Malay claim that Malay should be used at public meetings because this, rather than English, was the only common language of the people. An MCA Deputy Minister was later faulted for adding a few words in Mandarin after reading a speech in Malay.[3] Members were expected to use correct Malay grammar and pronunciation when speaking in Parliament, and were rebuked or mocked if they made mistakes.[4] The same level of proficiency was required in state and municipal politics.[5] But other professionals whose activities were more private and consultative and less in the public eye exploited their relative freedom to choose the language that corresponded to the social setting. In medicine, for instance, the extent to which Malay was used depended very much on the communicative setting, function of the interaction, and identities of the participants. A Deputy Dean of the Medical Faculty of Universiti Kebangsaan Malaysia reported that

> although Bahasa is frequently used between patients and students, reports on cases and examinations are often recorded in English. Furthermore, discussions between patients and students are in Bahasa, while discussions between students and lecturers are in English. The faculty's major problem is that it has yet to set up a policy in implementing the use of Bahasa.[6]

Doctors might also switch languages when speaking and writing. Announcing that all case notes would soon have to be written in Malay, an official explained that when a doctor spoke to a patient from some other language group in the national language and then wrote his case notes in English, serious misinterpretations arose. Moreover the non-Malay doctor often had problems communicating with Malay-trained nurses.[7]

The lawyer's case was different yet again. In this chapter we see how factors in his professional environment encouraged or discouraged the use of Malay. His purposes in communicating are distinguished here in terms of the degree of discourse control that he wished to exercise. By discourse control is meant the addressor's enforcing upon the addressee his choice of topic, criteria of relevancy, and choice of the linguistic structure of the interaction. The balance of control varies in different types of discourse and at different points within a discourse. The term "negotiation" is employed here to indicate the process by which the balance of control is determined. As a simple example, the speaker who asks the most questions gets the most answers and thus considerable control. But as soon as he allows the other participant to take a questioning role, the balance of control is shifted.

The costs to the listener or reader who resists this control are severe. A soldier cannot claim lack of interest as a defence for not obeying a properly phrased order given by a superior officer. The car owner who does not bother to read his insurance policy before signing it has only himself to blame if the company fails to accept his claim. Danet lists a range of stylistic and syntactic features of "frozen" legal language (see Joos 1961 for a classification of styles; and see also Crystal and Davy 1969, chapter 8; Swales 1982, Bhatia 1983, Swales and Bhatia 1980). In the following fragment selected from the Malaysian data, we need only note the complexity of clause relationships, technical terminology (e.g. line 16, "pursuance"), and terminology which carries a technical sense in law and non-technical sense in other registers (e.g. line 9, "effected"; line 19, "indemnity").

(C) *Non-Contribution Clause* This Insurance does not cover any loss or damage which at the time of the happening of such loss or damage is insured by or would, but for the existence of this Policy, be insured by any other existing Policy or Policies except in respect of any excess beyond the amount which would have been payable under such other Policy or Policies had this insurance not been effected. Exclusion of Legal Liability in respect of Passenger: Notwithstanding anything to the contrary contained in Section 11 - 1 (a) of this Policy it is hereby understood and agreed that the Company shall not be liable in respect of death of or bodily injury to any person (other than a passenger being carried by reason of or pursuance of a contract of employment) being carried in or upon or entering or getting on to or alighting from any motor vehicle in respect of which indemnity is provided under this Policy at the time of the occurrence of the event out of which the claim arises.

(Car Insurance Policy issued by a Malaysian company, 1981)

The reader of the Policy is not invited to make his own interpretation of its meaning and application, and no concessions are made to his particular circumstances. No attempt is made to persuade or to win his sympathy. On the other hand, this degree of legal obfuscation is by no means extreme; Danet, 1980 quotes and analyses one famous sentence from a Citibank loan form that runs to 244 words. (pp. 476-84). This form is also discussed in Charrow and Crandall 1976; and see Shuy and Larkin 1978 for further comments on the linguistic problems encountered in interpreting insurance policies.

The second fragment below is very different. It comes from a legal aid interview and is consultative in style. It typifies the way in which speakers communicate in a non-formal setting when they do not have a close personal relationship. Unlike the invented "telephone - bathroom" fragment quoted in chapter 1, the context is not taken for granted, and speakers supply background and contextual information. Although Speaker A has control of information about the law (the provisions of the Evidence Ordinance), Speaker B enjoys a monopoly to information about his own circumstances. The speakers negotiate the application of the institutionalised law to the particular set of facts. Legal terminology is restricted to nominal groups (line 12; "the presumed dead person"; line 15, "affidavit"),

(D)

Speaker A: How about your sister?

Speaker B: Sister also no idea. She has to help the family also.

Speaker A: You know why all these things I ask you because under the section er hundred and eight it must be close relative you know close relative so that most likely person would be your sister lah Lim Yoke Heng and your father.

Speaker B: Ah huh. Cik er Lim Yoke Heng can be a witness, because she's a family member.

Speaker A: Er. That one is a close friend but under the division of the section er under the Evidence Ordinance it says it must be nearest er closest to the presumed dead person. But never mind that, we will see what happens when the twenty-eighth. If the judge says you need a further affidavit from Lim Yoke Heng then we just have to include another affidavit. Just in case.

Speaker B: So do I have to bring the two witness to KL?

Speaker A: Your father. Your father has to come.

Speaker B: And then how about the other one must come also?

Speaker A: Must come.

(Kuala Lumpur Legal Aid Bureau Interview: 17 September 1981)

The frozen policy made no concessions to the reader's dialect. He was expected to adapt his use of English to the writer's needs, rather than vice versa. But the interview illustrates the standard Malaysian English dialect. (Note line 6, the emphatic "your sister lah"; line 20, "Then how about the other one must come also?") (For discussions of Malaysian English see Tongue 1979, Platt and Weber 1980, Wong 1981).

The Directive did not enforce the use of Malay in other than official legal interactions, and any such attempt would have failed. Where lawyer and client consulted in private and out of the public gaze, they quite naturally interacted in their most fluent common language. This underlines the point made in the previous chapter, that the implementation of language policy encouraged the development of a bilingual profession where the choice of language was determined by context and function.

The third fragment which follows shows that we cannot generalise from the interview to argue that all spoken Malaysian legal English employed the standard Malaysian variety. The cross-examination exemplifies the lawyer's courtroom language (other than when making a frozen summation.) It demonstrates the formal style and is ostensibly designed to inform. Although counsel addresses his utterances to the witness, in practice he elicits agreement to a body of information intended for the benefit of the court. He is professionally detached. His implicit disapproval and disbelief of an opposition witness' testimony makes as much a display designed to persuade the court as does his approval of his own witness, and it masks his real feelings (even if they should happen to coincide). The formal style tends to grammatical complexity, and to a technical or sub-technical vocabulary (in line 1, "authority"; in line 3, "acted in accordance with"; in line 14, "you are bound to inform"). The witness accedes to the formality; in line 2, "yes your honour" is addressed to the magistrate, not counsel, with the proper nomination. In (E) and (F) the witness is appearing for the defendant in a civil suit.

(E)

Counsel: Do you have authority to issue this letter?
Witness: Yes your honour.
Counsel: You acted in accordance with. Will you please look at this agreement please. You acted in accordance with clause nine of this agreement.
Witness: Yes your honour.
Counsel: I shall read the relevant part of the agreement. . . . So you acted in accordance with clause nine of the agreement. Does it state anywhere in the agreement that you must inform the purchaser of the change.
Witness: As far as the contractual agreements between the developers and ourselves?
Counsel: No I'm asking if you are bound to inform the purchaser of any change in this contractual agreement.
Witness: No.
Counsel: So you are not bound to inform the purchaser?
Witness: Yes.

(Kuala Lumpur Magistrates' Courts: 16 March 1981)

The witness is obliged to accept the convention that his function is to answer questions, and to give direct answers. He cannot refuse this role.

(F)

Counsel: So that means your house was completed in accordance with plans and you accepted it?
Witness: I erm.
Counsel: No answer my questions. You accepted it or you

did not?
Witness: (inaudible)
Counsel: Did you accept it or did you not accept it?
Witness: Yes.

(Kuala Lumpur Magistrates' Courts: 16 March 1981)

Counsel attempts to appropriate the witness's information, often by questions asked in declarative form (in (F), lines 1-2; "So that means . . . and you accepted it?"), and the witness may be reduced to acknowledging counsel's interpretation (in (E), lines 6, 17, 19). Danet refers to research in Danet and Kermish (1978) and Danet et al. (1980) to show that in the court room "declaratives are the most coercive because they tell more than they ask ("You did it . . .")" (p. 521). Contrariwise, Sinclair (1975) demonstrates that when the factor of control is not significant, declaratives permit the greatest range of interpretations. The declarative "I'm looking for the zoo" can be interpreted first as a statement and elicit a simple acknowledgement ("Hm"), or as a *yes/no* question ("Yes, that's it") or as a *wh-* question ("Down the road and on the right") or as a command (the addressee take the addressor). The context determines which interpretation is appropriate (see also Mead 1980, Ch.4).

Nevertheless, there is always an element of negotiation present. Counsel is permitted to suggest the the witness is lying, but not to inform the court that he is certainly lying, or that the truth of the matter is certainly x. The court enjoys the prerogative of making up its own mind, and when the witness holds out against counsel's version of the truth, counsel must allow this. In (G), line 3, he resorts to reminding the court of its prerogative and duty to adjudicate.

(G)
Counsel: You say he was there?
Witness: He was there.
Counsel: The court will decide.
Magistrate: (PAUSE) Right.
Counsel: (PAUSE) Yes. If you read that letter that I gave you just now . . .

(Kuala Lumpur Magistrates' Courts: 16 March 1981).

The preceding analysis provides support for a categorisation of fragments (C), (D) and (E) in terms of the degree of control imposed by the lawyer on the layman and the degree of negotiation between the parties.

	(frozen) Policy	(consultative) Interview	(formal) Cross-Examination
	(C)	(D)	(E)
Control by the lawyer:	very high	low	high
Negotiation between parties:	very low	high	low

The fragments examined here show that the management of a successful examination or cross-examination that both elicits appropriate evidence and persuades the court requires considerable forensic and linguistic skills. The lawyer would naturally choose to conduct it in the language which seemed most likely to maximize his control of the witness and to minimize the element of negotiation. In the confines of the courtroom, the intentions of the language planning authorities counted for less than did the language of the witness, the lawyer's own language, and the decision of the court. Where all, or a significant majority of participants in the trial were non-Malay, the court had little incentive to employ Malay. The final provision of the Directive, that the use of Malay should not injure the cause of justice, meant that the participants in a trial had greater opportunity to determine the language of use than did, say, the participants in a political debate or pupils in a school classroom.

We go on to look at the courtroom constraints that affected the use of Malay or English and determined how far the courts implemented the language policy. The argument focuses on the procedure followed in Malaysian Magistrates' Courts which handled about ninety-six per cent of all court business. (See also Mead 1985 for a detailed analysis of the discourse of these courts.) The discourse was influenced by three features:

- Procedure followed the English model.
- The magistrate was obliged to take notes of all proceedings in his own hand.
- Extensive use was made of interpreters.

We need deal only cursorily with the first two. Lind and O'Barr (1979) write that the English adversary system

> has given rise to legal procedures and norms which provide that the judge . . . should delegate authority over the presentation of evidence and arguments concerning the case to attorneys who are partisan advocates of the conflicting viewpoints in the legal disputation. (p. 69)

Counsel constructed the body of evidence by asking questions of his own witnesses in direct examination and of the other side's witnesses in cross-examination. His success in deriving the answers he wanted depended on his capacity to ask questions that exercised control (Harris 1982). Regulations affected the degree of control that he was permitted to exert. He was allowed to ask leading questions, which suggested the answer to the witness, throughout cross-examination. He was allowed to ask leading questions only when examining his own witness in respect of introductory matters—the witness' name and address, for instance; about matters which were clearly not in dispute; and to secure an express denial of an allegation.

The Directive only ostensibly affected proceedings by enforcing that, so far as possible, they should be conducted in the medium of Malay rather than English. The functions that the lawyer performed in court were rooted in English tradition and precedent. To the extent that he depended on a literature in order to interpret these, and the literature was English, he was likely to resist using Malay.

The second and third features were peculiar to the Malaysian system. The magistrate, who sat alone, was obliged to take notes of all proceedings. (In the English system, the clerk rather than the magistrate is responsible for taking notes, and only such as are necessary. See The Magistrate, vol. 37, no. 9, September 1981, p. 130; and also Practice Directions, 15 January 1954. (All England Law Report 230; 1954.) These notes usually represented the evidence in first person narrative form, although counsel could request that the evidence be recorded in its original question and answer form. An example is given in (H).

(H) PW2 - Z. binte M. R. being affirmed, states in Malay: 20 years. Jalan Laut, Johore Baru.

I am now unemployed. I am Thai. I knew Accused (identified). Accused was my husband now "pasah." I marry Accused 9 month ago.

We got married in Thailand. (Certificate shown.) This is the marriage certificate—produced as P2. I was brought to Malaysia 3 days after marriage.

Accused brought me to Machang in Kelantan. Before marriage I do not know what Accused was doing. At Machang I did not do anything. I stayed in Machang about 3 months. At Machang I do not know what my husband was doing. He left me. I did not know where he went.

After 3 months he came back.

(Johore Baru Magistrate's Court: 1976)

This regulation directly affected proceedings insofar as they were paced at the speed of the magistrate's speed or writing, and he was obliged to keep checking his understanding. The Directive required that the magistrate write his notes in Malay, and this served to reinforce Malay as the spoken medium. There was also an important indirect effect. We have seen that more and more magistrates were Malay. Errors in his notes gave grounds for appeal, and when English was the language of the court, the Malay magistrate tended to procrastinate in writing up his notes in English and incorporating them into his official Record of Proceedings. This led to delays in appeal procedure. The switch to Malay tended to alleviate this problem.

The third feature, which deserves more attention, was the use of interpreters. An interpreter in a Magistrates' Court doubled as court clerk. He was, however, almost without training in either role. He certainly could not be compared to the clerk in an English Magistrates' Court, who had most probably qualified as a solicitor and was responsible for explaining the law to his most probably lay justices. The Malaysian clerk had only an organizational role similar to that played by the English court usher, and once a case was underway and no interpreting was required, he was underemployed.

His lack of professional training as interpreter significantly effected the implementation of the law, and goes some way to explaining the deterioration in the court system. We need to see how he performed this function. Lang lists five types of improper interpreting in his discussion of local courts in Papua-New Guinea (1976): derogatory remarks made by the interpreter of his client, misinterpreting due to carelessness, misinterpreting resulting from "the substitution of a command by the reasons for that command" (p. 350), careless paraphrasing, misinterpreting due to auditory misperception. My Malaysian data do not give instances of the first category. However examples of misinterpreting arising from careless paraphrasing and auditory misperception were common, as in the fragment below. The plaintiff claims maintenance (see also (K) below).

(I)
Counsel: Is it a squatter house? (INTERPRETER/PLAINTIFF: MALAY INTERACTION)
Interpreter: It is a wooden house.
Counsel: No, no, is it a squatter house?
(INTERPRETER/PLAINTIFF: MALAY INTERACTION)
Interpreter: Yes it is a squatter house.
(Kuala Lumpur Magistrates' Courts: 8/1/1982)

One advocate told me of a case in which he was prosecuting a very elegant Malay woman accused of murdering her English lover, when he noticed that the nails of her right hand were cut unusually short. His question in English "I notice that you keep good care of your appearance" lost its force when translated as equivalent to "I notice that you keep good care of Europeans." In a second instance a Chinese advocate who had an elementary knowledge of the minority dialect spoken by his witness began to suspect that the interpreting was going awry. He pointed out of the window and asked "What color is that car?" The reply came back "Ford Cortina 1968."

But simply to catalogue errors misses the point. The untrained interpreter laboured under extraordinary circumstances of which he was as much victim as cause. His relationships with counsel, the magistrate, and the witness demonstrated the faults of the system in detail. Quite probably, his mastery of the informal codes was much greater than of the formal codes. Only an unusually courageous interpreter would tell the court when he could not cope. One Tamil-

English-Malay interpreter of eleven years' standing told me "an interpreter with guts might say the witness does not understand, could you ask in different words?" but this happened infrequently.

Counsel might be unaware of, or cynically exploit, the difficulties involved in translating even apparently simple sub-technical, non-legal terms; for instance, before "rear right-hand window" can be rendered in Tamil, the witness' spatial relationship to the car must be established. When the interpreter appeared to be entering into a prolonged negotiation in order to clarify the point, he might exploit the opportunity to make a show of self-righteous impatience. He might not understand the extent to which different forms of sentence construction in the two languages bedevil any attempt to precisely render emphasis. My informant represented counsel's attitude to the effect that "If I ask the question angrily, you must also put it angrily to the witness." Counsel's own lack of forensic expertise created additional difficulties; "lawyers like to ask long questions at a time. If they liked to ask precise questions, that would help a lot."

At its worst, the use of interpreters reduced the implementation of justice to a lottery in which the outcome was determined by factors outside the control of both the layman, who did not speak the language of the court, and of the court itself. Speaking from the English bench on an English case, Justice Roxburgh commented:

> Theoretically an interpreter is merely a mouthpiece and not an advocate at all, but in fact when an interpreter translates counsel's questions into the language of the witness, what happens is that rules of evidence are broken and unless counsel or the judge knows the language, they are powerless to prevent it. (Re Treba Mines, Ltd., *Weekly Law Review,* vol. 1, p. 24, 1960.)

The rules were broken in cross-examination when the restrictions imposed by a leading question were negated and a leading question might be rephrased in non-leading form (vice versa in direct examination). For example, from a civil suit:

(J) 1	Counsel:	No there was no question of you dealing with the old insurance company, you agree? (INTERPRETER/WITNESS: PUNJABI INTERACTION)
	Counsel:	You agree or not?
	Interpreter:	I was not familiar with the procedure.
	Counsel:	Doesn't matter, doesn't matter, it was third party insurance.

(Kuala Lumpur Magistrates' Courts: 27 April 1982)

In this instance the witness was allowed to avoid giving a yes/no reply and instead replied as though in response to an open question "Why did you not deal with the old insurance company?"

The magistrate retained control of the ultimate right to adjudicate, but circumstances obliged him to relinquish control of the immediate interaction. The interpreter acted as a mediator:

> In negotiations there may be, but not invariably is, a third party who, though he has no ability to give a judgement, acts in some ways as a faciliator in the process of trying to reach agreement. This is the mediator. (Gulliver 1977, p. 15)

Gulliver allows for the interested mediator. Indeed, very few mediators may be entirely disinterested. The Malaysian courtroom interpreter was formally interested insofar as he was an office of the court and informally insofar as he depended for future employment on at least a display of impartiality. Because he served a system that was designed to maintain balance between conflicting parties, he paradoxically upheld his own long-term interests by disinterested participation.

He demonstrated his disinterest by precise translation to the extent that he used the first person pronoun. Examples are given in (J) and (K).

(K)

Counsel: Now how many of your children are working? At the time of your husband's death how many of your children are working? (INTERPRETER/PLAINTIFF: MALAY INTERACTION)

Interpreter: At the time of my husband's death two children were working.

Counsel: Now. The two children who were working. What were they working on? (INTERPRETER/PLAINTIFF: MALAY INTERACTION)

Interpreter: They were working as factory workers, your honour.

Counsel: So I would be correct to say that at the time of our husband's death these two children were contributing? (INTERPRETER/PLAINTIFF: MALAY INTERACTION)

Interpreter: Yes your honour it would be correct to say that at the time of my husband's death they were contributing.

(Kuala Lumpur Magistrates' Courts: 8 January 1981)

In practice, however, this ideal of how the interpreter performed his role did not always apply. When the interpreter and witness belonged to the same community and neither counsel nor court officials belonged to that community or spoke its language, the interpreter enjoyed relative immunity. He might then be less concerned to serve the cause of justice than that of his communal fellow. Very much a junior in the legal world, he may have trained in legal procedures for only two months. He did not share the high status of the magistrate and lawyer, and had no reason to give the profession the same degree of loyalty. His community was likely to retain his greater sympathies, and these were readily given expression.

According to my informant, "the interpreter sees his responsibilities more on behalf of (his) client than on behalf of the court." For instance, he might help an accused construct a plea in mitigation, or in extreme cases, make it for him. "When he is asked if he has anything to say, the accused says 'Nothing, I leave it to you.' So the interpreter asks 'Where do you work, how many children do you have?' . . . (But) magistrates have their own stereotypes. So they don't believe there is much truth in it. . . . The magistrate might say 'Well, if you have no job and six children you will be better off inside.' Then the accused is taken by surprise and doesn't know what to say, because it is a creation of the interpreter." An example of an apparently "assisted" plea is given below, where the interpreter violates the convention that the words of the person in the box should always be translated in first person. Sociolinguists will note that the third person pronoun expresses solidarity here, a phenomenon not accounted for by R. Brown and Gilman (1960) in their classic study. In (L), the accused is pleading mitigating circumstances.

(L)

Magistrate: Where is he from. (INTERPRETER/ACCUSED: URDU INTERACTION)

Interpreter: He is a Pakistani. He wants (inaudible) in order to get back. He was in Bangkok in one month and then came to Malaysia. He had no relatives here. He was desperate because he had no means to support himself . . .

Magistrate: What were you doing in your country? (INTERPRETER/ACCUSED: URDU INTERACTION)

Interpreter: I was working as a foreman and before that in Saudi Arabia.

Magistrate: Saudi Arabia he says and then he had a telegram from his relative asking him to return home; . . . (INTERPRETER/ACCUSED: URDU INTERACTION) Your honour he says he is a first offender and asks for a lenient treatment. (INTERPRETER/ACCUSED: URDU INTERACTION) I have been under arrest for twenty-two days and my visa has expired and I pray your honour may make arrangements for me to be sent back to my country.

(Kuala Lumpur Magistrates' Courts: 8 January 1981)

In (M) the magistrate actively participates in this slide from social distance to solidarity. His question in line 12, "How long has he known you?" is reformulated in lines 19-20, "How long has he known him?"

(M)

Magistrate: What do you want to say in mitigation? (INTERPRETER/WITNESS: MALAY INTERACTION)
Interpreter: Some papers your honour which he has prepared to the court.
Magistrate: My God. Who wrote these for you? (PAUSE) There is a letter included. (INTERPRETER/WITNESS: MALAY INTERACTION)
Interpreter: One of his friends in the prison.
Magistrate: Hm?
(INTERPRETER/WITNESS: MALAY INTERACTION)
Interpreter: One of his friends in the prison.
Magistrate: How long has he known you? (INTERPRETER/WITNESS: MALAY INTERACTION)
Interpreter: It's more than six months.
Magistrate: (inaudible) (INTERPRETER/WITNESS: MALAY INTERACTION)
Interpreter: He promised that he will not do it again in future.
Magistrate: It's a very serious one you know. (PAUSE) How long has he known him?
Interpreter: More than six months.
Magistrate: More than six months. Tell him I will give him a chance you know? He'd better change. If he appears before me again (inaudible). One year's imprisonment from the appearance, ha? Don't do it again.

Kuala Lumpur Magistrates' Courts: 24 March 1981)

In the fragment below, the interpreter answers counsel's question (line 5) without referring it back to the witness. Apparently the extended interaction in line 2 had provided the interpreter with all the information needed.

(N)

Counsel: What day did you visit this depot? (INTERPRETER/WITNESS: PUNJABI INTERACTION: 6 EXCHANGES)
Interpreter: I went there after the Chinese New Year.
Counsel: Yes what date, what date?
Interpreter: I can't remember.
Counsel: You can't remember.

(Kuala Lumpur Magistrates' Courts: 27 April 1982)

I also observed one case in which the interpreter and two accused participated in an interaction consisting of at least twenty-seven separate speech turns, at the end of which the accused changed their plea from no guilty to guilty. The magistrate neither initiated this interaction, nor closed it, nor commented on its outcome. True, the interpreter had assumed a role that far exceeded her statutory responsibilities, but on the other hand her initiative had shortened the court's work considerably.

The witness distinguished between the interpreter and other officers of the court, and readily exploited the interpreter's capacity to mediate. He directed his contributions towards the interpreter. He employed a different range of para-linguistic gestures and was more likely to introduce new topics, interrupt, and give irrelevant information than if speaking directly to counsel or the magistrate. In other words, he followed the conventions of everyday conversation rather than those of the courtroom. Bergman (1979) notes that

> for that increasingly small segment of the population that has not attended law school, direct answers to questions are not natural. (p. 235)

Moreover the relationship with the interpreter was apparently perceived as an invitation to revert to "natural" conversation. Second, the witness who possessed at least a passive understanding of the language of the court was at a double advantage. He had the opportunity to process the question when it was put by counsel and a second opportunity when the interpreter reformulated it.

Thus far we have considered evidence of the use of an interpreter working to the advantage of the witness. However, this was not always the case. I observed one trial in October 1980 in which the unrepresented accused, magistrate, prosecuting office, and witness were all Malay, yet English was employed as the language of the court. The prosecuting officer's questions were put in English, interpreted into Malay, and the witness' evidence was then interpreted back into English. One lawyer explained this to me as a relatively common practice intended to "confuse an unrepresented person who doesn't speak the language." No doubt it did, and given one calculation that in 1973, 34.3 per cent of accused persons claiming trial in Kuala Lumpur Magistrates' Courts were unrepresented (Lim Heng Seng 1975), such tactics must have produced a healthy conviction rate. No doubt the Malay layman with any experience of being at the mercy of a legal system practised in a language that he did not understand applauded the Government's decision to implement the language policy in the courts, whatever objections the profession might put up.

The data indicate that the extensive use of English in the courts before the Directive was issued and the dependence upon interpreters were detrimental to the ideal of an impartial system of justice based upon rules of evidence, and were the cause of great inefficiency. One last example illustrates the point. It comes from a *New Straits Times* report of the trial for murder of the Culture, Youth, and Sports Minister at the time.

> After the Attorney General had read a portion of the statement, recorded in Bahasa Malaysia, Mr. Justice Hashim commented that there was a problem of defence counsel not understanding what was being read. He then asked what should be done about it.
>
> Mr. Jagjit Singh, leading counsel for Datuk Mokhtar Hashim, the first accused,

> suggested that copies be made for them. The suggestion was supported by Mr. Manjeet Singh, leading counsel for Rahmay Satiman, the third accused, but the judge replied "not at this stage."
>
> He then suggested that Encik Abdullah read the statement and the interpreter translate it for the benefit of defence counsel.[8]

Counsel's inability to use Malay complicated court business and called into question procedural conventions. For as long as the status of the two languages was ambiguous, counsel could gain considerable tactical advantage by feigning ignorance of one or the other.

The Directive had the effect that the interpreter's work load was immediately lessened (although his services would be required for years to come by those non-Malays who had left school before 1982). An interpreter informant suggested that he expected his role to change. Rather than between the witness on the one hand and counsel on the other, he would find himself mediating between a Malay-speaking witness and court, and a counsel whose grasp of the language was still shaky.[9] Counsel placed in this novel psychological relationship with the witness would derive further stimulation to learn the language.

The magistrate decided whether Malay or English should be employed as the language of the court. But the witness had the right to request the services of an interpreter. We have seen the procedural problems that could arise when evidence was interpreted. Hence the decision made by the witness who preferred not to use Malay influenced the implementation of the language policy.

Thus far the chapter has examined the extent to which the activities performed in the courtroom and the decisions made by the various participants determined the choice of language. We conclude by seeing why the use of Malay legal terminology posed conceptual problems for the lawyer and gave him further reasons for dragging his feet over the language policy.

The lawyer was expected to employ a Malay legal terminology. The *Dewan Bahasa dan Pustaka* had produced a list of 2,000 legal terms in 1971, and planned a further 2,000 in 1982 and 1,000 more thereafter.[10] But even a total of 5,000 terms could not encompass all areas of legal expertise. (The medical profession suffered from a different problem. The 24,000 item terminology permitted greater latitude of expression,[11] but lacked authority. A university dean explained that a number of organisations were independently producing terms, and the lack of standardization meant, for instance, that "appendix" was translated as "appendiks" in higher institutions but as "usus buntu" in school texts.)[12]

The extent of the terminology did not guarantee its currency. When circumstances demanded the use of terminology, the lawyer who did not know the official term was inclined to invent his own—a solution from which the doctor might demur.

> The spirit of what one lawyer wished to convey was not lost when she ungrammatically said "tidak halangan" for "no objections." While "bantahan" is the correct term for objection, her denial of any obstruction was picturesque and vividly clear nevertheless.[13]

But this was unlikely to be a permanent solution. Organisations concerned with developing a national language for nationalising purposes or with protecting the national culture and language against foreign influences are commonly insistent on the need to counteract language "pollution." Besides the *Dewan Bahasa dan Pustaka* jealously protected its monopoly to decide correct usage.[14]

Secondly, the lack of a precise Malay term or a known alternative was overcome by code-switching.

> Courtroom fumblings in Bahasa have made hilarious reading, but the language problem is not nearly as formidable as it initially seemed. . . . No presiding member batted an eyelash when legal phrases in English were thrown into the context of Malay sentences. "Saya kan apply for cost." "I will apply for costs" was accepted without demur the first week the ruling came into force.[15]

Counsel had grounds for according official terminology a low priority. Evidence from at least one other multilingual court system suggests that precise translations of terminology may be relatively unimportant. In his discussion of interpreting problems faced by the European Court of Justice, L. N. Brown (1981) writes

> The Court of Justice commonly prefers a teleological or schematic interpretation of a provision of Community Law; the wording, of course, is not ignored, but primary importance is not given to "*les termes.*" (p. 321)

He refers to Ehlermann's (1976) three explanations for the relatively minor significance given to the actual wording. Community law leaves a multitude of legal concepts undefined; the conditions under which Community law was and is prepared are not conducive to careful drafting; Community law is frequently framed in a language other than the mother tongue of the draftsman. As Malaysian law moves away from English law, at least the first two of these three factors are increasingly likely to apply in Malaysia also.

When appearing in a run-of-the-mill case (for instance, robbery, possession of dangerous drugs, and traffic offences), counsel's need for technical terminology was minimal. When examining a layman, his first consideration was that his questions should be comprehensible. The fragment from a civil suit given in (K) illustrates the point. Counsel and the interpreter (when speaking English) employ a formal style, but the cross-examination is conducted throughout without recourse to legal terminology.

In conclusion, we look briefly at the different explanations given for the reason implementation of the language policy in the courts proved to be so difficult. The significance of the lack of Malay translations of legal literature has already been discussed and need not detain us further.

The Director General of the *Dewan Bahasa dan Pustaka* claimed that the main obstacle to the use of Malay was the lawyer's refusal to learn the language.[16] Given the communal composition of the Bar, this argument would seem to carry some weight. But we have seen that when professional issues were at stake, communal loyalty counted for relatively little. Moreover the profession knew which side its bread was buttered on; when the Government underlined the need for Malay language skills by announcing that in 1984 all members of the Bar would have to pass a language test in order to practise,[17] lawyers were not slow to take the hint. Short-term courses in legal Malay were organised by the Bar in Johore[18] and then in Kuala Lumpur, where more than half the Bar were registered. The first course in Kuala Lumpur attracted a class of 250.[19]

A Malay magistrate (quoted in (M) told me "sometimes I don't know a term (in Malay) and so I prefer to use English." If a Malay preferred to interpret the law in English, it is scarcely surprising that non-Malays shared the same feeling. Lawyers objected to the new terminology on the grounds that it was "too vague for arguing through legal technicalities."[20] Contrariwise, a language planner claimed that

> a technical or scientific term always has a correspondence in another language. . . . In this case, then, *atom* should bear the same concept in English as it does in Malaysian and Indonesian or any other language no matter what its phonological representations are in these languages.
>
> (Asmah Haji Omar 1979, p. 105)

The reformers appeared to hold, first, that meaning was fixed by the linguistic item that carried it, and second, that an equivalent item could be formulated in a second language and be applicable to precisely the same range of referents. We may hypothesize that the reformers" backgrounds reinforced this view. Islamic culture teaches that language has divine origins, is precise, and hence no useful distinction can be drawn between the dictionary definition of a word and its significance (Laffin 1975, pp. 56, 72-76). Secondly, Malay schools relied heavily on rote learning (Abdullah Taib and Mohamed Yusoff Ismail 1982, p. 111), and pupils were not encouraged to question the conventional meaning of a text. The lawyer, on the other hand, had learnt to distinguish meaning as object (or artefact) and meaning as act (Danet 1980, pp. 455-57; also Bates 1976, p. 8). Meaning is created by the interactional process, and the appropriate connotation denoted by a specific term derives from the situational and linguistic contexts within which it is used. His training told him that precedent was a significant determinant, and much of his practice boiled down to reinterpreting conventional meaning in the light of different circumstances.

It may have been the case that in physics the concept "atom" was invariable, whatever the context. But this was not true of legal concepts. The "frozen" Insurance Policy quoted in (C) demonstrates the extremes of grammatical prolixity to which the legal writer was driven in his quest to pin down a single possible meaning. That is, terminologies had different statuses as vehicles of meaning in different fields. Hence, translated or invented equivalent terminologies in another language were also likely to have different statuses. The acclaim given to a Malay terminology of physics did not guarantee that a Malay legal terminology should be of equivalent value, or that the lawyer would be as willing and able as the physicist to implement this aspect of the language policy. The lawyer's primary concerns in using Malay were to hit the appropriate formal style and to control his witness as effectively as when using English. The solutions proposed by the language planners were couched in terms of formal systems—spelling, grammar, and terminology (Asmah Haji Omar 1979), and did not take account of the contextual determinants of language functions and their realisation.

The language policy was formulated by language planners and politicians, but in practice was implemented by various professional groups, each of which had its own interests to protect and whose use of Malay or English was constrained by its different relationships to its audience and its different professional activities. This chapter has shown that the relative ease with which policy was enforced in education or politics, for instance, did not guarantee a simple switch to Malay in the legal system where other conditions prevailed. Considerable use has been made of linguistic data. The data demonstrate the notion of control in legal procedure, and show the importance of discourse organisation as a tool for applying control. They also show how the interpreting process impaired legal procedure and compromised the administration of justice. This discussion substantiates the use of discourse description as a tool for doing social science analysis.

Finally, it has been suggested that the status of terminology in law did not correspond to its statuses in other fields. That is, the language policy assumed different significances in different fields. This discussion of synchronic variation is extended in the next chapter by a review of diachronic variation. The language policy changed over time, and the policy of 1957 was not the same beast in 1967 or 1983. This development held important implications not only for the legal system but for the future of Malaysian society as a whole.

CHAPTER FIVE

Conclusion

In the course of this monograph the focus has narrowed from an examination of the political setting and culture policy that influenced language policy, to the implementation of languagepolicy within the education system and the significance of its success and failure there, to its implementation within the legal system, until finally we have seen the use of Malay determined not only by policy makers but also by participants in the courtroom. At each stage of the argument the factors that delayed or favoured the use of Malay as the language of the law have been examined. We have elaborated the themes of continuity and discontinuity in official policy, and discussed the pressures of communal and social ferment that determined new priorities.

The months under examination (late 1980 to early 1983) witnessed the coming to power of a new administration and an apparent heightening of the political temperature. The events of this period have been analysed in terms of a historical context dating from before Independence in 1957. At the time of writing, we are already in a position to trace forward their significance. For instance, the causes of the conflict that erupted between the traditional Malay rulers and the administration in late 1983 and the impotence of the MCA in 1984-5 were seeded well before, and have been examined here. But no attempt will be made to bring the story up to date. Recent events do not significantly modify the thesis. The partial patching up of relations with the UK and the growing doubts over the "Look East" policy in 1984-5 indicated a slight swinging back of the pendulum,[1] but the general tendency to create a Malaysian identity was not seriously compromised.

This short conclusion similarly eschews exact prediction. But it does suggest that the desire to break with the past had not yet been exhausted, and seemed likely to further affect the development of social institutions including the legal system. Thus far we have emphasized the element consistency in the language policy, manifested over time in different fields of activity, particularly in education and the law. We now take up the latent theme of development within the philosophy guiding the language policy and the implications this had for further change.

The constitutional contract had given the lion's share of political power to the Malays and had not attempted to restrict non-Malay economic power. The contract had been agreed to in a mood of idealism and optimism, and the language policy had seemed the appropriate tool to create an environment of national unity without seriously compromising the cultural or economic integrity of any one community. But in the decade after Independence very little was done to implement the education policy and to create the structures of unity. The 1969 riots demonstrated the emptiness of political power without economic muscle, and showed that trusting to providence was insufficient. Throughout the next decade, the language policy changed from being an instrument of national integration to one designed to impose Malay cultural and economic supremacy. It was intended to complement the New Economic Policy in educating a Malay middle class and hobbling the non-Malays. We have seen that these policies achieved only limited success.

The evidence shows that Dr. Mahathir's administration gave particular emphasis to the culture policy as an instrument for assimilating the non-Malays. Moreover the previous administration had already begun to move in this direction. Datuk Hussein Onn was reported to have said in 1980 that

> the New Economic Policy, the National Education Policy, and the National Cultural Policy were the basis for national unity.[2]

Initially then, the problem of achieving national unity had been tackled by a national language policy applied within the education system; then, after 1969, by education and economic policies designed to prevent a recurrence of the riots and to express national ideology in terms of Malay priorities. The events of 1980-1983 showed culture policy increasingly employed as the means to achieve these ends. Defined in terms of Islam, it touched on all aspects of social life and subsumed and determined education and economic policies. The cultural tail now wagged the language dog. Language policy was used to reinforce "official" Malay values within the Malay community and to impose them on the non-Malays. The non-Malays were overcoming the burden of not speaking Malay, and were now handicapped by their lack of participation in Malay and Islamic culture.

Most non-Malays were unlikely to convert to Islam. Hence superficial analysis might suggest either that UMNO anticipation of creating a united and tranquil Islamic polity showed a hopeless disregard for realities, or that the hurdle of culture had been erected as a means of permanently locking non-Malays into their role of "resident stranger" (McVey ms. 1983). The facts indicate that we should take this second interpretation one step further. Historical and cultural factors led the administration to adopt an increasingly pro-Malay stance, but it was still obliged to turn a blind eye to many infringements of policy by the non-Malays. This strategy of muddling through—in essence not so different from that followed before 1969—held the nation together but at the cost of heightening the sense of uncertainty and hysteria.

The principles of establishing Malay political supremacy and economic parity and creating a sense of national unity and identity at first enjoyed considerable support; the specific policies adopted to realise them were increasingly incompatible. A host of illustrations have demonstrated friction between Malays and non-Malays and within the Malay community. The Government failed to formulate a convincing ideal of Malaysian society that justified yoking policies to discriminate in favour of the Malays and policies to create national unity. This led to a growing lack of correspondence between the official analysis of events and the realities of ordinary life, and so the contradictions widened. Evidence of failure was greeted by officialdom with extravagant claims of actual or imminent success, a raising of targets, and the suppression of criticism. We have seen that after 1969 the language policy was increasingly employed as a means of enforcing Malay cultural values rather than of binding the communities, and this establishes the point in general terms. A few further instances reinforce this diagnosis of pathology.

We have noted that the New Economic Policy was designed to give Malays thirty per cent of share capital and ownership by 1990. In 1980, the Federal Territory Minister responded to

> certain groups who had criticized the Government for the fact that in the past five years bumiputra share in the economy had only reached two per cent.
>
> "They are very doubtful that, based on this evidence, bumiputras could hope to achieve 20 per cent by 1990," he said.
>
> "However, they have not taken into consideration the human factor, where with the correct leadership and guidance, attitudes could be changed and more achieved."[3]

A few days later, however, at the Third Bumiputra Economic Congress, a delegate

> proposed that the bumiputra share of the economy be raised from 30 per cent by 1990 (as targeted under the New Economic Policy) to 51 per cent.
>
> This proposal, a spokesman said later, was received "enthusiastically" by the other delegates.
>
> The congress later adopted a resolution which said: "In achieving the target of at least 50 per cent bumiputra participation in the economy by 1990, bumiputras must increase their savings quickly . . . there must be an incentive scheme to enable bumiputras to increase their savings."[4]

The subsequent Bumiputra savings scheme was reserved for Malays only. But non-Malays circumvented this regulation by paying willing Malays a percentage to invest in their names. Similarly, the "Ali Baba" system, by which non-Malays financed Malays to register ownership and to act as front-men, overcame the Malay near-monopolies in such industries as transport. The non-Malay success in exploiting these economic loopholes defused an explosive situation. At the same time it vitiated the Government's policy of developing a class of Malay entrepreneurs. In effect the Government had handed a cake to the Malays, who had passed on a sizeable slice to the non-Malays. Immediate crisis was diverted, but the frustrations felt by all communities were exacerbated.

The same patterns were repeated in the implementation of language policy. Officially, the policy had succeeded. Datuk Musa Hitam claimed that

> Malaysians must accept the reality that Bahasa Malaysia is no longer the language of one race but that of all Malaysians. . . . It is "our" language in every sense of the word. . . . It is not far-fetched for me to say that we have successfully revived Bahasa Malaysia, both physically and mentally, in an amazing short period.[5]

Two academics credited this "success" to the

> feeling of unity that this language has instilled in the hearts and minds of the people of Malaysia as a national language. It has managed to maintain its position as a lingua franca and as an official language among the different races.[6]

Their suggestion that Malay had "a bright future as an international language at ASEAN conferences,[7] and in the United Nations; the Malacca Chief Minister claimed that "We can never be regarded as being truly successful if the language does not achieve this objective."[8] (Malay speakers, including Indonesians, totalled about 150 million.)

These dreams perhaps offered an escape from the problems of creating linguistic and cultural unity at home, but the doubts remained. One observer noted:

> Datuk Ismail Hussein, head of the University of Malaya's Malay studies department and president of the Malaysian Writers Association, said in a recent interview that while statistically the use of Malay has increased, "from a quality perspective the trend is worrying. There is little feeling among Malay intellectuals for the language. Usually they use Malay because they feel forced to do so."[9]

Even the Director General of the *Dewan Bahasa dan Pustaka* claimed that while the language had been used as the medium of instruction in schools and universities, its use outside these places had been minimal. He said English was still preferredin social and informal gatherings, in the private sector and in economic and industrial activities.[10]

The language planners responded to these difficulties in creating a Malay speaking language polity by enforcing use of the language with greater severity. We have noted the restrictions placed on the professions, and the pressures applied to recalcitrants. Initially the use of Malay as official language had not been intended to apply within the private sector, but now businessmen were criticized for failing to follow the public sector.[11] Senior teachers blamed the low percentage of Higher School Certificate examination passes in Malay not only on the exodusof the best students abroad but also on Ministry of Education examiners. A headmaster said that there must be "something wrong somewhere."

> "I certainly do not think my boys did that badly in the Bahasa paper. I wonder whether those people (the authorities) had suddenly raised the standard of Bahasa even higher . . . at their own whim," he said. Another principal who faced a similar situation in his school was more blunt.
>
> "The examiners who corrected the paper must be sick, real sick," he said.[12]

The conflicts beneath the surface of Malaysian society were not yet entirely expressed and the need to resolve the contradictions never fully faced, except perhaps by academics.[13] In the 1982 elections, the National Front had gained almost 90 per cent of the 154 parliamentary seats and 312 seats in eleven state assemblies.[14] These figures suggested a far greater degree of satisfaction with official policy than in fact existed; 37 per cent of the Malay electorate voted for opposition parties. As the wealthy urban Malays grew apart from their cousins in the east coast kampongs and the drive to unity among the communities faltered, the need to impose cultural hegemony increased. And the problems of imposing it correspondingly increased. A Malay lawyer writing under the headline "The press in a climate of fear" reminded his readers that when Dr. Mahathir assumed power

> he took a number of measures which gave rise to popular expectations that his government would be more liberal and democratic. The previous administration had suffered widespread local and international criticism over its record on human-rights violations.[15]

But, he continued, these hopes had been disappointed. His fears for the future echoed a columnist writing in the Star; (his emphasis)

> *Dissent and the right to complain is the unalienable right of every citizen in this country or any other country that practises parliamentary democracy. It is only a totalitarian country, whether of the right or of the left, which ruthlessly stamps out all forms of dissent.*[16]

The Government made increasing use of the media in order to propagate its interpretation of Malay and Malaysian values.[17] Newspapers and journals were under considerable pressure to abide by guidelines; at different times in 1982-3 both the UMNO-controlled *New Straits Times* and the MCA-controlled *Star* incurred official displeasure and were temporarily suspended from Ministerial briefings. Television and radio gave increasingly greater emphasis to official information;[18] note, for instance, the Government's concern that the growth of the video industry and the import of foreign video films were leading many Malaysians to "skip" television and radio announcements and "vital programmes on national ideals and policies."[19] When propaganda failed to contain discontent, the government could always resort to the grim apparatus of the Internal Security Act and the Sedition Act.

The drive to enforce Malay values in all social institutions provides basic evidence for arguing that the implementation of language policy within the legal system was not intended as an end in itself. The syndrome discussed in this chapter of responding to signs of policy failure by enforcing even stricter controls gives further cause to assume that the reluctance of the legal profession to jettison its common law traditions will not be ignored forever. It seems logical to suppose that the legal system will become steadily more local in character, and that the Directive will prove to have been a major influence in this development. This inference might be disputed on the ground that in the Meiji period Japan applied translated German law, and that King Chulalongkorn based the Siamese system on translated French law; and so the use of the national language did not necessarily presage the development of an indigenous system. But German and French influences were chosen deliberately by the rulers of free countries in the first stages of modernization. Our data suggest that the Malaysian government was considering the possibilities of creating an indigenous alternative to the colonial system of English Common Law.

Of course a Malaysian system cannot be imposed overnight nor will English influences be as quickly uprooted. A hybrid will be developed, and the Government will compromise between the extremes— neither politically expedient—of maintaining the legal system as at present (although Malay-medium) and immediately applying the Shariah system. In time this hybrid will become less English and increasingly Malay. As new interpretations are made of the Constitution, the traditions that the legal profession guards so jealously will be pruned away. This fits with Hooker's (1978) general prediction for the area.

In the final analysis it is likely that the hybrid form of law will prove the most suited to the needs of Southeast Asia (p. 14). But this masks serious political problems. Formulating a strategy to implement a progressively more Malay legal system and to secure its popular acceptance presents the same difficulties as enforcing the culture policy to which it is subordinated. The culture policy has been posed in terms of Malay privilege, and demonstrating that legal policy can serve to unite the communities in the national interest will severely test the Government's political adroitness.

The picture painted here might not seem to represent the development of a secure society, united and confident of its identity. On the other hand, memories of 1969 acted as a terrible warning of what could happen again if solutions were not found and the economic and educational gains made since 1957 exploited to the general betterment. Energy, talent, and goodwill were not lacking.

In the eyes of the 1983 UMNO leadership, the problems of building a Malaysia that enshrined Malay supremacy and exorcised the nightmare of communal riot could only be solved if the Malays were united among themselves and the non-Malays persuaded to accept Malay values. The policies discussed in this monograph were not intended merely to assimilate the non-Malays; they were also intended to assimilate the Malays. How far such policies could be successfully implemented remained, and still remains, an open question.

Afterward

The first draft of this monograph was completed in early 1984 and the second draft in early 1985. Since then, Malaysian social and political structures have been buffeted by a succession of crises. While the final drafts were being corrected in October 1987, Dr. Mahathir's government was embroiled in a number of political disputes which bore directly on issues raised in the body of this monograph. Quotation from the regional press indicates that many of the problems apparent in the years under examination, 1980-1983, are still very far from resolution.

1. The text suggested that the government will make increasing efforts to impose policy on the legal system.

Since 1986 UMNO and Dr. Mahathir have been "concerned" over the way several judicial decisions have gone against the executive branch of the government. High Court judge Harun Hashim has been at the centre of the ensuing debate over the separation of powers. *From Asiaweek:*

> Together with several prominent Malaysians— including Tunku Abdul Rahman, the nation's first prime minister, and Perak Sultan Azlan Shah and Tun Suffian, both former lord presidents—Harun also recently called for a review of the Malaysian Constitution. He has also proposed a radical reform of the Senate, the Malaysian Parliament's upper house, and suggested that the country's emergency laws, many of which have been in force since the war against communist guerillas during the 1950s, be allowed to lapse. Again, without mentioning any names, Mahathir said in response that judges should restrict themselves to implementing the law, not forging or changing it. . . .
>
> *Asiaweek* understands that in recent weeks senior government officials have repeatedly stressed to Barisan leaders the necessity to ensure that judges "do not step out of line," as one UMNO leader put it. Says a top Barisan official: "We have been left in no doubt that some sort of action is being contemplated." Another says that "several alternatives have been discussed," including the use of sections 125 and 127 of the Constitution, which relate to the sacking of judges and parliamentary motions to discuss their conduct and censure them.
>
> ("Of Politicians and Judges," October 16, 1987.)

2. The text noted the problems faced by the MCA in representing the Chinese and remaining loyal to their government partners, the importance that

the Chinese assign to their schools, divisions within the Malay community, and the increasing intolerance of dissent.

On October 27, police arrested "over 20 people" including Lim Kit Siang, his DAP colleague Karpal Singh, and Chandra Muzaffar under the Internal Security Act. By November 3 the number had swelled to 93 and included opposition politicians, members of interest groups, and a handful from the MCA, Gerakan, PAS, and even UMNO. The majority were Chinese.

> The only common thread, analysts said, is that they appear to have periodically opposed several government policies or offended the UMNO leadership's sensibilities. (*The Asian Wall Street Journal*. "New Detentions Net Malaysia's Chief Dissidents," October 29, 1987.)

All public demonstrations were banned and the printing permits of three journals, including the *Star*, were revoked. Tunku Abdul Rahman commented, "I'm very angry with what's happening. This is no democracy. This way is towards dictatorship." (*Asiaweek;* "A State of Shock," November 6, 1987.) *Asiaweek* explained

> The authorities say the arrests were necessary to pre-empt any interracial confrontation amid growing friction between the country's Malay and Chinese communities. Emotions have been running high in recent weeks, mainly because of the assignment by the government of non-Chinese-educated teachers to Chinese-language schools, a move hotly opposed by many ethnic Chinese.

There was reason for supposing that unrest and the decision to detain had also been influenced by government and party divisions. An analyst told *The Asian Wall Street Journal* that

> "UMNO is flexing its muscles to intimidate its partners. . . . On the other hand," he added, "the Malaysian Chinese Association is seeking to regain its identity" as the champion of the ethnic-Chinese.
>
> The MCA, a member of the ruling National Front, has been deeply divided by the Chinese primary school issue, which has put the party at odds with its traditional political partner, UMNO. ("Malaysia Arrests Powerful Critics in Police Sweep," October 28, 1987).

The UMNO detainees included party officials who had been aligned with Tengku Razeleigh Hamzah, the former trade and industry minister who had narrowly failed to wrest the leadership from Dr. Mahathir during the party's triennial elections in April and was continuing to contest the elections in the courts.

An UMNO rally had been planned for November 1 to celebrate the party's 40th anniversary. Some 500,000 Malays were expected to converge on Merdeka stadium. A crowd this size would have reflected Dr. Mahathir's control of the party and the failure of Tengku Razeleigh and Datuk Musa Hitam to take power.

According to *Asiaweek,* Razeleigh's supporters had sensed this and were trying to turn the rally to their advantage by stirring up racial tensions.

> Plainly, the quickest way to defuse the tension was to call off the rally. But Mahathir associates had reasoned that a postponement of the public meeting would have been read as a sign of weakness. The swoop, says one UMNO insider, gave Mahathir a way out. "If the rally had gone on and only a portion of the estimated 500,000 people had turned up, Mahathir would have lost face," he says. "If any untoward incident had taken place, Mahathir would have been blamed. There were far too many risks involved."
>
> But some in Mahathir's camp had been saying openly for days that any incident would be to the PM's advantage. A deteriorating law-and-order situation could justify the declaration of a state of emergency and rule by decree. Mahathir's associates say their boss was against the idea of imposing emergency rule. Says one UMNO leader who supports Razeleigh: "Mahathir had two options: allow the rally and if things got worse declare a state of emergency, or cool tempers and find a good justification for the cancellation of the rally. He chose the second. The swoop was part of the whole package." (*Asiaweek,* ibid.)

The Nation (Bangkok) editorialised

> It is extremely likely that Mahathir had reached a state when he was not able to control his own UMNO and with the MCA and the opposition parties pitching in, he decided to create a crisis situation. If that is the case, Mahathir has committed the worst blunder in his political career. ("Has Mahathir Offset or Created Racial Tensions?" October 29, 1987.)

3. Observation indicates that the national language policy has still not been fully implemented in the court system.

October 4, 1987
Graduate Institute of Business Administration, Bangkok.

Abbreviations

BN	Barisan Nasional (National Front)
DAP	Democratic Action Party
HSC	Higher School Certificate
IMP	Independence of Malaya Party
MARA	Majlis Amanah Rakyat
MCA	Malayan/Malaysian Chinese Association
MCP	Malayan Communist Party
MIC	Malayan/Malaysian Indian Congress
MTUC	Malaysian Trade Union Congress
NEP	New Economic Policy
NF	National Front
PAP	People's Action Party
PAS	Parti Islam Se Malaysia
PMIP	see PAS
POL	Pupils' Own Language
SUPP	Sarawak United People's Party
UKM	Universiti Kebangsaan Malaysia
UM	Universiti Malaya
UPM	Universiti Pertanian Malaysia
UMNO	United Malays National Organization
USM	University Sains Malaysia

Notes

Chapter 1

1. *Bahasa test a "must" for lawyers soon,* ***Star,*** 21 October 1981, Kuala Lumpur.
2. *Butterworth Court starts using Bahasa,* ***Malay Mail,*** 1 October 1981, Kuala Lumpur. "Lower courts in Butterworth have been instructed to use Bahasa Malaysia *as far as possible,* although it is not compulsory yet." "Magistrates have been told to use Bahasa whenever possible as long as justice is not hindered."
3. *Bahasa takes a leap in legal work,* ***Malay Mail,*** 26 February 1981.
4. *Bahasa Malaysia for all lower courts soon,* ***Star,*** 10 June 1981.
5. *Wider use of Bahasa in lower courts,* ***Star,*** 16 June 1981.
6. *Lower courts may use Bahasa by end of year,* ***New Straits Times,*** 16 June 1981, Kuala Lumpur.
7. *Use of Bahasa won't hurt trials: Suhaim,* ***New Straits Times,*** 25 September 1981. " 'The use of Bahasa Malaysia in the lower courts in two years time should not worry anyone as the same high standards in the trials will continue,' Deputy Education Minister Datuk Haji Suhaimi Datuk Haji Kamaruddin said today." "Describing the court as the 'last bastion of the English Language,' he said that as long as the use of Bahasa did not stand in the way of a fair trial, there was no reason why it cannot be used in the courts."
8. Bartholomew quotes Blackstone's ***Commentaries*** Vol 1, on the introduction of English Law in settled colonies. "But this must be understood with very many and very great restrictions. Such colonists carry with them only so much of the English Law, as is applicable to their own situation and the condition of an infant colony. . . . The artificial requirements and distinctions incident to the property of a great and commercial people . . . are neither necessary nor convenient for them and therefore are not in force." (Blackstone, p. 107).
9. *Translate Court Judgements* ***Star,*** 26 January 1983. "Chief Justice Tan Sri Mohamed Salleh Abas . . . said most legal authorities had to be quoted in English during court hearings as they were basically of English descent."

   " 'We are using about 90 per cent of laws from England which are expressed in English and thus it is impossible for us to transform everything into Bahasa Malaysia immediately,' he said."

   Other estimates ranged as high as 99 per cent. ***Suara Peguam*** (newsletter of the Penang Bar Committee) noted "the British precedents of 99% of our laws." (October 1980).

10. *No wish to stop students going abroad,* ***New Straits Times,*** 25 November 1980.
11. *Only systems useful to us: PM,* ***Star,*** 6 April 1983. " 'Although the Malaysia Inc. system is based on the Japanese practice of close co-operation between the public and private sectors, there will be certain differences,' Datuk Seri Dr. Mahathir Mohamed said."

    "He claimed this was because of differences between Malaysian and Japanese society. For instance, they have a homogeneous society and do not face the problem of racial economic disparity. Therefore we have to ensure that policies like the New Economic Policy are not abandoned when the concept is implemented. There may also be other systems used by the Japanese which may not be suitable for use here—for instance from the cultural aspect— and we will not use them."
12. *Ten years of success,* ***Sunday Star,*** 29 March 1981, Kuala Lumpur.
13. But some observers expect this development of the Malay middle class to engender increased conflict. Note *The dilemma of unifying a multilingual society,* ***Far Eastern Economic Review,*** 17 November 1983, Hong Kong, by James Clad. "But against this picture of increasing adaptability the leader of the Aliran reform movement in Penang, Chandra Muzzafar, told a seminar this year that an emergent Malay middle class alongside an established non-Malay middle class may lead to 'worsening communal relations even though conflict over language is now muted.' "
14. "Definitions of a Malaysian culture beyond an awkward fusion of ethnic trace elements remains a rarefied University-bred commodity." S. W. Gardner, "Ethnicity and Work: Occupational Distribution in an Urban Multi-Ethnic Setting in George Town, Penang West Malaysia." (Ph.D. thesis, Berkeley: University of California, 1975), p. 24.

    See also, Juliet Edmonds, "Religion Intermarriage and Assimilation: The Chinese in Malaysia," *Race* x. 1968.
15. *5 groups that have different ideas,* ***Sunday Star,*** 19 December 1982.

    Dr. Firdaus Abdullah of the University of Malaya classified the groups in his paper entitled "Politics of national culture in Malaysia."

    The iconoclasts regarded Malay culture as merely one of the many ethnic cultures in the region and wanted the Chinese, Tamil, and English languages given official status, although agreeing on Malay as the national language. This cause was advocated by an opposition party but there were also secret champions in the ruling Barisan Nasional.

    The conservative fundamentalists wanted national culture to be based wholly and categorically on Malay culture and Islam.

    The "anglicised" and "westernised," secularists came from the elite upper class and and upper middle class and were separated by a wide social and psychological gap from the common people.

The idealists, felt that Malay and Islam had a deeper and more important bearing on the history and social development of the country than other languages and religions.

The last group the "progressive nationalists," comprised those who thought along the lines of official policy. Because their views had been assimilated into or coincided with policy, they could be regarded as the foremost faction, according to Dr. Firdaus. Bernama (The official Malaysian Press Agency).

16. *Sanusi: Groups out to disrupt writing of Malays,* ***New Straits Times,*** 26 November 1980.
17. *MP: Counter deviant teachings,* ***New Straits Times,*** 13 November 1980.

    "Deviant teachings a threat to security" reminder, ***New Straits Times,*** 3 November 1980.
18. *Casino ban on Muslims,* ***Star,*** 18 January 1983.
19. *Morals contract for MARA loans,* ***Star,*** 24 March 1983.
20. *Committee to review Syariah Court Act,* ***New Straits Times,*** 17 November 1982.
21. *More power for kadis, syariah courts,* ***Star,*** 30 March 1983. "Acting Prime Minister Datuk Musa Hitam . . . said: 'The Government is aware of the implications of a misunderstanding of Islamic laws which can lead to fear among the people. As such, a number of high-level committees have been set up to study the various aspects of Islamic laws and their implementation.' "

    "Datuk Musa said there was a committee to look into changes in the syariah courts, a committee to formulate Islamic family laws and a committee to formulate laws on information and systems. To overcome the problem of misunderstanding, it was important to give the right information to the people. 'Islam forbids extremism,' he said."

    "In Malaysia, extremists have appeared who make use of their religion and their activities can also lead to disunity among Muslims."

    See also, *Support for move on syariah courts,* ***New Straits Times,*** 31 March 1983.
22. *Steps taken to enhance powers of syariah courts,* ***New Straits Times,*** 31 March 1983.
23. *Separate laws for Muslim families sought,* ***New Straits Times,*** 27 January 1981.

    See also, *More power for kadis, syariah courts,* ***Star,*** 30 March 1983.
24. *Bill to better enforce Islamic law passed,* ***New Straits Times,*** 14 December 1982.

    See also, *$300 fine for Muslim women who don't dress properly,* ***New Straits Times,*** 8 January 1983.
25. *Take rear seat to avoid Khalwat, women told,* ***New Straits Times,*** 24 January 1983. "Earlier, Haji Abdul Kadir bin Mat, 50, and Esah binti Ismail, 40, told the court that the road where Azizah was arrested by religious officers was busy with people and that there was light from street lamps and the main gate

of the General Hospital.

In his submission, Datuk Wan Mustapha said that the charge was defective because to prove *Khalwat,* there had to be proximity in an enclosed place.

As to suspicion, he said it should be reasonable and not based on the whims and fancies of religious officers. Otherwise, he said, all women in Kota Baharu would be arrested."

26. *No lion dance for national culture: Adib*, **Star,** 20 November 1982. " 'The lion dance cannot become part of the national culture,' Acting Culture, Youth, and Sports Minister Encij Mohamed Adib Adam said."

"He told Mr. Lee Lam Thye (DAP-Kuala Lumpur-Bandar) that this was because the lion dance could not be accepted by all the people in the country though it formed an important part of Chinese culture. Replying to the original question by Datuk Michael Chen (BN-Bruas) he said that the national culture policy was based on three principles.

They must be based on the culture indigenous to this region, the features of other cultures must be suited to the national culture, and that Islam must be an important element."

"Based on these three main principles, the national culture will eliminate racial cultures. It is now in the process of evolution and it will comprise the basic culture and the different ways of life of the races in Malaysia, said Encik Mohamed Adib."

"He said that Malaysia needed to have a liberal attitude towards the country's rich cultural heritage. He told Datuk Lee Kim Sai (BN-Ulu Selangor) that there were two ways in which cultural practices can become features of the national culture."

"One was when such practices became the norms of the people and the other through legislation like the prohibition of polygamous marriages among non-muslims."

27. *Kit Siang tells PM: Review cultural policy,* **Star,** 21 December 1982.
28. *Ministry to set up Silat Council,* **Star,** 13 December 1982.
29. *No lion dance for national culture: Adib,* **Star,** 20 November 1982.
30. *Gov't. told: Don't ignore reality of multi-racial society,* **Star,** 21 November 1982.
31. *Yee Pan: Let cultures evolve naturally,* **Sunday Star,** 22 November 1982. "MCA national deputy president Datuk Dr. Neo Yee Pan . . . said that a culture imposed through legislation would be artificial and have difficulty finding acceptance among the people."

" 'Culture is the crystalisation of the way of life of a particular community,' he said."

32. *San Choon: Understand the national culture,* **Star,** 8 December 1982.
33. *Pooling efforts for national culture,* **New Straits Times,** 21 December 1982.
34. *Gov't. pledge on culture to non-Malays,* **Star,** 24 January 1983. "The Government today assured non-Malays that their heritage would not be 'belittled'

when a national culture is formulated. Deputy Minister in the Prime Minister's Department, Encik Anwar Ibrahim, is giving this assurance, said that although the Malay culture would form the core of the national culture, 'the cultural heritage of those outside the Malay world will not be ingored.' "

35. *Why others should not worry about Islamic gov't,* ***New Straits Times,*** 8 December 1982. From Saad Hashim "Non-Muslims in Malaysia should not be unduly worried about Government efforts to inject Islamic values into the Government administration because their religions too, want the same thing. The Parliamentary Secretary to the Foreign Affairs Ministry, Encik Abdul Kadir Sheikh Fadzir, said 'As far as I know, every religion frowns upon things like drinking, gambling, and so on. The non-Muslims therefore need not feel worried about this new policy. He said the Government firmly believed that Islam has the answers to the problems faced by the country. This policy was not thought out to compete with PAS nor is it a policy of hypocrisy, opportunism for political expediency,' he said."
36. *Morals law next?* ***Sunday Star,*** 12 December 1982. "Your morals may soon be regulated by the law. It could be an offence to be caught necking at lovers haunts.

    Religious leaders of various communities are helping government officials study the possibility of drawing up what would be a Morals Law aimed at safeguarding the individual's moral values. It would apply to all people of all races and all religions.

    'The proposed law will not be based strictly on Islamic laws but will encompass the philosophies, tenets, and theologies of other religions including Buddhism, Christianity and Confucianism,' said Datuk Haji Mohamed Nasir, Minister in the Prime Minister's Department, who heads the special committee drawing up the law."

    See also, *Support for move on syariah courts,* ***New Straits Times,*** 31 March 1983.
37. *Morals law gets mixed reaction,* ***Star,*** 13 December 1982. "There was mixed reaction over the proposal to implement a new Morals Law to safeguard individual moral values. . . . Some have described it as ridiculous while others pointed out that the new law could only infringe on the rights of citizens and invade their privacy. . . . Many of them have asked why such a law should be introduced at a time when the country's leaders were saying that the new administration was practising a liberal policy."
38. *Views on morals law "misconstrued,"* ***Star,*** 22 December 1982.
39. *The father of Malaysia calls for a halt,* ***Far Eastern Economic Review,*** 3 March 1983. In this climate of political uncertainty, a call on February 8 by former Prime Minister Tunku Abdul Rahman for the government to cease moves toward Islamisation, came like a breath of fresh air to non-Muslims. On the occasion of his 80th birthday party, hosted by Mahathir, the man who led the country to independence from the British warned that Malaysia must never become an Islamic state. The constitution, he said provided that Islam should only be the official religion. Later, the Tunku told the ***Review*** that the notion of

an Islamic state was untenable in a multi-racial country like Malaysia. The Tunku's call was therefore welcomed as the first real acknowledgement of deep-seated fears. And five days after his speech, another former Prime Minister, Tun Hussein Onn, expressed similar sentiments, also on the occasion of his birthday.

40. *Coping with the "fire,"* ***Asiaweek,*** 17 December 1982, Hong Kong.

41. *Non-Muslims should stand up for their rights,* ***Far Eastern Economic Review,*** 3 March 1983, Interview/Paul Tan Chee Ing. Interviewer: "What of freedom to worship in the sense of having a place to worship? As I understand it, the plan for the development of Kuala Lumpur envisages that by the end of the century the population of the city will be made of about 35% Malays, and 65% non-Malays, while sites for mosques and for non-Islamic churches and temples are in inverse proportion."

    "Absolutely right. The master plan allots 513 sites to Islam and only 220 to other religions. The number of mosques and suraus (mini-mosques) is due to increase by nearly 430%, each serving fewer than 1,500 Muslims, while non-Muslim churches and temples are due to increase by 370%, each serving more than 6,500 people."

    "What of burial grounds?"

    "We were given absolutely none. Not only Christians but Buddhists and Taoists—none. Of course, this plan is not finalised and we have raised objections."

42. *Compulsory syllabus on Islamic culture,* ***New Straits Times,*** 1 November 1982. " 'The Government will issue a directive to make it compulsory for all universities and colleges to have a new education syllabus on Islamic culture from next year. The new syllabus will ensure that students fully understand the various aspects of Islamic culture,' Deputy Minister in the Prime Minister's Department, Encik Anwar Ibrahim, said at a ceremah at the conference of Ulamahs last night."

    "He said the move was in line with the Government's aim to set up an Islamic University in the country. He said it was also in line with Government efforts to instill aspects of Islam in the administration. He regarded those who opposed the move as having a narrow concept of nationalism."

43. Ibid., ***New Straits Times.***

    See also, *Universities to conduct Islamic course,* ***Star,*** 16 March 1983.

44. *Use* Jawi *on signboards call,* ***New Straits Times,*** 7 January 1983.

    See also, *Give Arabic the same status as English,* ***New Straits Times,*** 21 November 1980.

45. *Chinese are being left behind, says MCA leader,* ***Star,*** 9 March 1981.

Chapter 2

1. *Will HSC be as good as ever?* ***New Sunday Times,*** 15 October 1980, Kuala Lumpur.

2. *Chinese are being left behind, says MCA leader,* ***Star,*** 9 March 1981. "Mr. Kee Yong Wee, the deputy chairman of the Federal Territory MCA Liason committee, said . . . (that after 1969) various bodies like Pernas, MARA and SEDCs were formed and provided funds for an aggressive assault on commerce and industry. Education policies were also tailored to ensure that large numbers of Malays were educated. As an example, Mr. Kee said that the total allocations to Malay organisations for the Third Malaysia Plan were equal to more than half the paid-up capital of all the Malaysian companies listed on the Kuala Lumpur Stock Exchange. 'It is also apparent that today it is virtually impossible for non-Malays to obtain transport licenses, timber licenses or oil exploration rights,' he added."
3. *The role of education in Malaysia,* ***Star,*** 31 August 1982.

   For a study of the upward mobility of Malays through education, see also Christine Inglis, *Educational Policy and Occupational Structures in Pan-Malaysia,* in Issues in Malaysian Development, Jackson, J. C., and Rudner, M., eds. (Kuala Lumpur: Heinemann, 1979), pp. 205-32.
4. *Hamdan: Don't neglect English,* ***Star,*** 18 January 1981.
5. *Poor Bahasa has the students puzzled,* ***Sunday Star,*** 6 February 1983. " 'The survey showed that although lecturers are required to use Bahasa Malaysia for a certain fixed number of hours, some were not doing so,' said the secretary of the Bahasa Malaysia Society, Universiti Sains Malaysia, Encik Abu Kassim Mohamed. . . . Most of the lecturers are English-educated and are not well versed in Bahasa Malaysia."

   " 'Malay lecturers may be able to conduct lectures fluently in Bahasa Malaysia but they still face a problem expressing in a scientific and intellectual manner,' he said."

   See also, *The dilemma of unifying a multilingual society,* ***Far Eastern Economic Review,*** 17 November 1983, by James Clad.

   "Datuk Ismail Hussein, head of the University of Malaya'a Malay studies department and president of the Malaysian Writers Association, said in a recent interview that while statistically the use of Malay has increased, from a quality perspective the trend is worrying. There is little feeling among Malay intellectuals for the language, he said. 'Usually they use Malay because they feel forced to do so.' "

   "He continued: 'In the university, to write for a Malay-language paper almost suggests a derogation of status . . . there is a general sentiment that to write or be published in Bahasa Malaysia is not really academic.' Ismail also pointed to recent research showing that though university lecturers say they now deliver their lectures entirely in Bahasa Malaysia, in compliance with the law, 'the facts are otherwise.' "

   "Also prompting a reluctance among university staff, regardless of ethnic background, to develop their Bahasa Malaysia writing is a desire to be published in international—that is, mostly English-language-journals, to establish professional reputations."

6. ***New Straits Times,*** 21 December 1982.
7. *The role of education in Malaysia,* ***Star,*** 31 August 1982.
8. *Race gap is growing, warns Kit Siang,* ***Star,*** 18 July 1981, Kuala Lumpur, Fri. "DAP secretary-general Mr. Lim Kit Siang said tonight that racial polarisation was the foremost Malaysian problem in the 1980s. He said it was 'tragic' that the younger generation of Malaysians who are Malaysian-born and Malaysian-oriented are 'probably the most polarised and alienated.' "

   See also, *Meredeka U and the Mark Koding case,* ***Star,*** 17 February 1982. "High Court judge Mr. Justice Mohamed Azmi, who was hearing the case of Mark Koding (MP for Kinabalu) asked the prosecution if anyone was being charged for sedition in the Merdeka University case since it concerned the use of Bahasa Malaysia as well."

   "DPP Lamin Haji Yusuf replied: 'Not to my knowledge.' "

   "Judge: 'Does it mean that the new generation is more tolerant now?' "

   "DPP: 'I have my reservations.' "

   "Judge: 'No?' "

   "DPP: 'No, the new generation is more sectional, more factional and more racial.' "
9. *Sip Hon tells Chinese: Face the realities,* ***Star,*** 22 December 1980.

   See also, *Nation-building—through UMNO ties,* ***Star,*** 22 December 1980. Johore Baru, Sun. " 'The existing ties between the MCA and UMNO must be strengthened if the Chinese want a say, in running the country,' MCA central working committee member Dr. Gan Kong Seng said this evening."
10. Tan Sri Dr. Tan Chee Khoon, *On Chinese leadership and education,* ***Star,*** 20 August 1981.
11. *Chinese are being left behind, says MCA leader,* ***Star,*** 9 March 1981.
12. An advertisement for property at Rapat Damai, Ipoh, ***Star,*** 20 April 1983.
13. *MPs have no protection from sedition, says DPP,* ***Star,*** 18 February 1982.

    See also, *Merdeka U and the Mark Koding case,* ***Star,*** 17 February 1982.
14. *Gov't. won't divert from Bahasa objective: Khalil,* ***Star,*** 9 November 1982.
15. Tan Sri Dr. Tan Chee Khoon, *Other Languages must be taken more seriously,* ***Star,*** 16 December 1981.
16. *Language classes: it's up to the HMs,* ***Star,*** 9 November 1982.
17. *Memo says Pupils' Own Language classes in shambles,* ***New Straits Times,*** 14 March 1983, Kuala Lumpur, Sun. "The Pupils' Own Language (POL) programme in schools is in bad shape despite having gone on for 26 years, a memorandum on Mandarin and Tamil classes said."

    "Although the 1956 Razak Education Report specifically stated that POL classes were to be held in schools as long as the children asked for it, this is not so, it added."
18. *Bahasa not compulsory for all,* ***Star,*** 30 December 1981, Kuala Lumpur, Tues. "Chinese and Tamil National Type Primary Schools will not be involved in the

implementation of Bahasa Malaysia as the medium of instruction in all primary schools next year."

19. *3R's uproar—the truth and the supicion*, **Star,** 11 January 1982. "There is little doubt that government policy with regard to Chinese and Tamil primary schools has not changed."

    "But the Education Ministry's inept handling of the issues arising out of the introduction of the 3R curriculum has sorely taxed the goodwill of its supporters and increased the number of non-believers."
20. *Don't get it wrong says Minister*, **New Straits Times,** 8 January 1982.
21. *What MCA opposed about the 3Rs*, **New Straits Times,** 13 January 1982. "Calling the proposed implementation of the 3Rs a 'deviation from the Cabinet Report,' Datuk Lee said the MCA would do whatever possible to 'dissociate' itself from the implementation of the 3Rs in Chinese primary schools. He did not elaborate on what he meant by 'dissociate.' "
22. *MCA: 3Rs are fine but not this way*, **Star,** 13 January 1982.
23. *Sip Hon tells Chinese: Face the realities*, **Star,** 22 December 1980.
24. *DAP making language a political issue: Suhaimi*, **Star,** 19 March 1983.
25. *Rafidah blames guide book for the 3R controversy*, **Star,** 15 January 1982.

    "It is printed in Bahasa to enable all teachers to understand it but nowhere does it state that they have to teach in Bahasa. They will still teach in the vernacular languages. The medium of instruction will not be changed. But the controversy should not be used as an issue for politicking, especially by the Opposition. It is very sad that the Opposition wants to capitalise on this."
26. K. Don Buddhadsa, *Taxing time for teachers under 3R scheme*, **New Straits Times,** 7 April 1983. "Some teachers of first year 3R classes spend about eight hours at home daily preparing various teaching materials. The undesirable outcome: tired teachers who cannot give of their best."
27. *Murad: 3R teaching aids will not be translated versions*, **Star,** 1 May 1982.
28. *4 ways to teach 3Rs in Chinese*, **Star,** 7 January 1982. "The proposals—submitted jointly by the MCA, the United Chinese School Committee Association and United Chinese School Teachers Association are:

    - THAT all teaching materials, except English and Malay, be written in Chinese;
    - THAT the medium of instruction and examination for subjects other than English and Malay be Chinese;
    - THAT the subject matter of teaching materials on humanities, environment, moral education and music must reflect the characteristics of Chinese culture and values; and
    - THAT the teaching hours for English be increased."

    See also, *PM will keep his word: Chinese Teachers*, **Star,** 28 January 1982.
29. **Star,** 15 June 1982.
30. B. C. Bhattacharjee, *English medley*, **Sunday Mail,** 19 October 1980, Kuala Lumpur. "English as taught in our schools is deteriorating. It has become a

melange of Malay, Chinese and Indian languages directly translated into English with startling results."

See also, editorial, *Poor English*, **New Straits Times,** 28 October 1980. "Although the importance of English as a second language is acknowledged, the context in which it is taught leaves it with very few under-pinnings. The lack of social reinforcement and the lack of imaginative teaching methods and materials confine English mainly within the chalky walls of the classroom. The paucity of creative usage is further compounded by the fact that the langauge is not a compulsory exam subject."

See also, *Teachers urged to be more professional*, **New Straits Times,** 30 January 1982.

31. *Specially trained teachers for English classes*, **New Straits Times,** 1 November 1980.

    See also, *Shortage of English teachers*, **New Straits Times,** 27 July 1982.

32. *Don't be narrow-minded over language: Khir*, **New Straits Times,** 30 October 1980.

33. *Don't neglect English, says Raja of Perlis*, **New Sunday Times,** 28 June 1981, Penang, Sat. " 'The English language should never be neglected in our efforts to give primacy to Bahasa Malaysia,' University Sains Malaysia Chancellor, the Raja of Perlis, said today."

    "In industrial development and in the field of education itself, no one should ignore the importance of English as an international language, he added."

    See also, *Bilingual education system vital: Tunku*, **Star,** 18 December 1982, Alor **Star,** Fri. " 'A bilingual education system with English as the second language, is necessary to a developing nation like Malaysia,' former Prime Minister Tunku Abdul Rahman said here today."

    See also, *English is vital too: Rithauddeen*, Sunday **Star,** 19 December 1982.

34. *Gov't. won't divert from Bahasa objective: Khalil*, **Star,** 9 November 1982. " 'The Government will not divert form its objective to make Bahasa Malaysia the national and official language,' said Deputy Education Minister Datuk Mohamed. . . . He denied that the English language was still being given priority attention."

35. *Why S'pore is looking for foreign judges*, **New Sunday Times,** 11 January 1981.

36. *DAP's concern over the 3Rs*, **New Straits Times,** 8 January 1982.

37 *Vernacular schools "not ready for 3Rs*, **New Straits Times,** 2 January 1982.

38. *Kit Siang proposes "many languages, many cultures" movement*, **Sunday Star,** 31 October 1982. "DAP MPs and State Assemblymen must be the 'pillars' of the movement for a Malaysia of 'many language, many cultures' so that any attempt to impose a 'one language, one culture' policy would be abandoned, the party's secretary-general, Mr. Lim Kit Siang, said."

39. *3Rs will lower standard of pupils—DAP*, **New Sunday Times,** 10 January 1982.

40. *"Urgency" behind call for talks on 3Rs systems*, ***New Straits Times,*** 11 January 1982.

    See also, *DAP calls for a united front*, ***Star,*** 12 January 1982.

41. *Guild's protest against ban on 3R meeting*, ***Star,*** 15 February 1982.
42. *We'll tackle 3R issue our way: san Choon*, ***Star,*** 12 January 1982. "On DAP's call to convene an emergency session of Parliament, he said that the MCA would not support the proposal."
43. *MIC welcomes statement on 3Rs*, ***New Straits Times,*** 8 January 1982. "MIC President Datuk S. Samy Vellu . . . called on Malaysian Indians not to be misled by allegations that the 3R system was aimed at abolishing Tamil primary schools."

    See also, *Negative response to DAP's cable for meet on 3R*, ***New Straits Times,*** 12 February 1982, Kuala Lumpur, Mon. "The various political parties seem to be responding negatively to the DAP's cable to them to press for an emergency Parliamentary meeting to discuss the suspension of the 3R system in the national type primary schools."

44. For an interesting discussion of the early years of the MIC, see Rajeswary Ampalavanar. ***The Indian Minority and Political Change in Malaya 1945-1957*** (Singapore: Oxford University Press, 1981).
45. *Samy Vellu: Forge ties with others*, ***New Straits Times,*** 13 April 1981. "Datuk Samy Vellu . . . said more Indians should be encouraged to stand invited under one flag by joining the MIC 'for their ultimate survival here.' "
46. *Council unhappy over set-up of 3Rs*, ***New Straits Times,*** 16 January 1982.
47. *Tamil schools to go ahead*, ***Star,*** 13 January 1982, Kuala Lumpur, Tues. "Tamil primary school teachers will not support calls to suspend the implementation of the 3R system in national type primary schools."
48. *Vernacular schools won't be closed: PM*, ***Star,*** 10 March 1982.
49. *Pledge on schools*, ***Sunday Star,*** 24 January 1982, Kuala Lumpur. "Prime Minister Datuk Seri Dr. Mahathir Mohamed said today that although the Education Act empowers the Education Ministry to convert such schools to national schools, the Government had never done so of its own accord. 'Since Merdeka, only one Tamil school in Kelantan was converted to a national school at the request of the school and the parents,' he added."
50. *Stop stirring 3Rs issue*, ***New Sunday Times,*** 24 January 1982.
51. *Associations: We are not backing Gerakan*, ***Star,*** 2 April 1982.
52. *3Rs: Musa issues warning*, ***New Sunday Times,*** 31 January 1982, Sha Alam, Sat. "Stern action will be taken against those who try to use the new primary school curriculum (3Rs system) as an issue to create unrest in the country, Deputy Prime Minister Datuk Musa Hitam warned last night."
53. Ibid., ***New Sunday Times.*** "The Government took a serious view of the actions of these people who were using children to serve their own political interests."

    "Datuk Musa admitted that education was a sensitive issue which commanded the constant attention of the people."

" 'Unfortunately, education has been mixed with politics. It has also been linked to racial sentiments.' "

See also, *Don't mix education with politics, MCA told*, **Star,** 12 July 1982.

54. *Banned—V. David's 3R document,* **Star,** 13 March 1982. "According to a Government gazette, the printing, publication, sale, issue, circulation or possession of the document is prohibited as it is prejudicial to security and national interests."—Bernama.

    See also, *Cops say no to meeting on the 3Rs,* **Star,** 12 February 1982, Kuala Lumpur, Thurs. "Police have rejected an application to hold a meeting on the 3R curriculum at the Chinese Assembly Hall here on Sunday."

55. *3R pupils still can't recognise numbers,* **Star,** 9 April 1982.

    See also, *3R teacher ratio to be increased,* **New Straits Times,** 28 April 1982; *Better results under new 3Rs system,* **New Straits Times,** 29 October 1982, and *330 more teachers for Chinese primary schools,* **Star,** 6 January 1983.

56. *The resurgence of Chinese schools,* by K. L. Chew, **Star,** 26 May 1981.
57. *8,466 to sit for Chinese exam,* **Star,** 6 December 1980.
58. *How the system works,* **Star,** 12 December 1982.
59. *Varsity had support of 4,000 guilds: witness,* **Star,** 2 October 1981. ". . . from a Government survey conducted in 1978, there were more than 30,000 students in the Chinese secondary schools. Mr. Lim said that if the fees collected did not cover the expenses of these schools, the deficit would be covered by donations from the board of governors who raised the money from donations and 'from their own pockets.' From 1975 to 1980, a total of $32 million in donations was contributed by the Chinese community to make up for the deficits in fees and for development."
60. *How the system works,* **Star,** 13 December 1982.
61. *Chinese are being left behind, says MCA leader,* **Star,** 9 March 1981, Kuala Lumpur, Sun. "Over-zealous mis-implementation of the New Economic Policy by some Government officials will further polarise the races, an MCA leader said today. Mr. Kee Yong Wee said such mis-implementation led to feelings of frustration and deprivation among the Chinese, and these feelings were today so pervasive that the Chinese felt insecure and threatened.

    " 'When a Chinese feels victimised by unfair bureaucratic practices, he has little recourse for official remedy when the Government bureaucracy is almost 80 per cent dominated by Malays.' "

    " 'A result of this is the gradual disinterest of the Chinese community from the national affairs, and possible withdrawal of Chinese participation from civic affairs and business enterprise will further polarise the races.' "

62. In 1980, Christians formed about five per cent of the population—or ten per cent of the non-Muslim population. Approximately half were Catholic and half belonged to a wide range of Protestant Sects. See the (headline mutilated) by Tan Sri Dr. Tan Chee Khoon, **Star,** 10 December 1980. For an interesting discussion of local Buddhism, see V. Wee, in Riaz Hassan, ed., 1976, pp. 155-88.

63. *The Chinese education dilemma* by Chew Kheng Leng, ***Star,*** 13 December 1982.
64. *The role of education in Malaysia,* ***Star,*** 31 August 1982.
65. *59pc applicants for university entry were bumis,* ***New Straits Times,*** 13 April 1981.
66. *Malays form 62.3pc of new undergrads: Musa,* ***New Straits Times,*** 17 October 1980. "Universiti Kebangsaan took in 1,612 students for the academic year, of which 1,249 were bumiputras. Universiti Malaya took in 2,097, of which 1,062 were bumiputras. Universiti Pertanian took in 434 bumiputra students out of 565 new undergraduates. Universiti Teknologi had 163 out of 209."
67. *University paper chase now tougher,* by Lim Kaen Liang, ***New Straits Times,*** 14 November 1980. "Bumiputras were today told to regard the gradual increase in non-bumiputra intake in universities as a 'warning signal' that the paper chase will be more competition in the future."
68. *Varsities urged to adopt "open door" policy,* ***New Straits Times,*** 25 November 1980. "Wan Mohamed Najib bin Wan Mohamed (NF - Pasir Putch) urged the Government to defer implementation of the additional two per cent intake of non-bumiputras into the universities. He said it was prudent that this two per cent formula be implemented after 1990 when the objectives of the New Economic Policy were expected to be achieved. He said any move to implement the formula before 1990 would only under-mine efforts to raise the education and economic standards of the bumiputras."
69. *Education policy is divisive: Lam Thye,* ***Star,*** 1 April 1981. "DAP MP for Kuala Lumpur Bandar Mr. Lee Lam Thye . . . said that diminishing educational opportunities, especially for higher education, and the sense of insecurity felt by the majority of Malaysians about vernacular education formed two of the biggest educational grievances in the country."
70. *Is there a need for a sixth university?,* by Shaik Osman Majid, ***Sunday Mail,*** 20 December 1981.
71. Idid., ***Sunday Mail.***
72. Ibid., ***Sunday Mail.*** "Unfortunately, no one, least of all the Education Ministry, can provide the figures. Indeed, as one of the officials sheepishly acknowledged last week, it is only now that studies are being carried out to find out the actual picture of our students abroad. The foreign embassies which handle student applications provide some statistics but these are only approximate figures which, tallied up account for the 40,000 very often cited as the number of students abroad. Whether all are undergoing university courses is the $64,000 question."

    See also, *Sixth varsity is necessary, say dons,* ***Star,*** 17 December 1981.
73. *"When in need, hit the students,"* by Malcolm Rutherford, ***New Sunday Times,*** 23 November 1980.
74. *A home cure for culture shock,* by John Pillai, ***New Sunday Times,*** 26 October 1980.
75. *Varsity had support of 4,000 guilds: witness,* ***Star,*** 2 October 1981.

76. *Bar on appeal to Privy Council*, ***New Straits Times,*** 10 July 1982.
77. *Need for agency to help these schools*, ***New Straits Times,*** 20 November 1982.
78. Ibid., ***New Straits Times.***
79. *Is there a need for a sixth university?*, ***Sunday Mail,*** 20 December 1981.
80. *No wish to stop students going abroad*, ***New Straits Times,*** 25 November 1980, Kuala Lumpur, Mon. "The sending of Malaysian students abroad for higher education does not reflect on Malaysia's education system, in fact, it is helping the Government to make the system a success, the Dewan Rakyat was told today."

    " 'That is why the Government itself is sending many youths abroad to study,' Education Minister Datuk Musa Hitam said. By studying abroad, he said, the enrollement in local schools and institutions would be reduced, thus giving the opportunities to those who could not afford to go overseas. Replying to a supplementary question from Mr. Lim Cho Hock (DAP - Ipoh), he said he has two children studying overseas."
81. *Poor Bahasa has the students puzzled*, ***Sunday Star,*** 6 February 1983.
82. ***Star,*** 17 July 1981.
83. *Poor Bahasa has the students puzzled*, ***Sunday Star,*** Kuala Lumpur. 6 February 1983.
84. *Shortage of BM college texts can be solved*, ***New Straits Times,*** 5 October 1981.
85. *Indon ban unfair, says literary council*, ***Star,*** 21 December 1982.
86. Editorial: *Varsity books*, ***Malay Mail,*** 27 December 1980. "Translation requires books to translate. In many technical fields there simply is a dearth of local books in any language. Our scholars have not produced very much on Malaysian subjects in English. The lack of financial and promotional incentives, low royalties, inadequate provision for subsidies and secretarial assistance have all contributed to the unwillingness of academicians to become the vanguards of this national effort."
87. ***Star,*** 20 November 1982.
88. *"Education policy too successful." It may need to be reviewed: Musa*, ***Star,*** 11 April 1983.
89. *Bahasa deadline for ALL our primary schools*, ***New Straits Times,*** 29 December 1981. "Education Minister Datuk Dr. Sulaiman Haji Daud . . . said the enforcement of Bahasa Malaysia as the *lingua franca* of the nation was successful. However, he expressed dissatisfaction with the pupils performance, particularly Malay pupils, in the subject."

    See also, *Bahasa: Malay students poorer*, ***Star,*** 29 December 1981, Kuala Lumpur, Mon. " 'Malay students have a poorer command of Bahasa Malaysia than students of the other races,' Education Minister Datuk Dr. Sulaiman Daud said today."
90. *Ten years of success*, by Peninjau, ***Sunday Star,*** 29 March 1981. "Between 1970 and 1980, the bumiputra share of employment rose from 32 to 40 per cent in the secondary sector (manufacturing, mining, construction and

transport) and from 42 to 47 per cent in the tertiary sector (trade, banking, public administration and other services). Surveys also showed that the average income of Malays increased at a slightly faster rate than the Chinese and Indians, thus narrowing the gap between the ethnic communities a little. For instance, the Malay mean income was $172 per household per month in 1970 (or only 65 per cent of the national mean average of $264) but this rose to $309 in 1979 (or a slightly increased 67 per cent of the national average.)"

91. Federation of Malaya Legislative Council Debates, ***Official Report,*** July 11, 1957 (Kuala Lumpur: Government Printer, 1957). Quoted in Von Vorys 1976, p. 137.
92. *Chinese are being left behind, says MCA leader,* ***Star,*** 9 March 1981. "A result of this is the gradual disinterest of the Chinese community from the national affairs, and possible withdrawal of Chinese participation from civic affairs and business enterprise will further polarise the races."
93. ***Star,*** 15 December 1980.

Chapter 3

1. National Language Act, 1967. Clause 8.
2. ***Star,*** 19 June 1981.
3. *Gov't. move to beat the legal backlog,* ***Sunday Mail,*** 2 November 1980.
4. *Butterworth court starts using Bahasa,* ***Malay Mail,*** 1 October 1981.
5. *In the dark over Bahasa in courts,* ***New Straits Times,*** 13 October 1981.
6. *First High Court Case in Bahasa,* ***Star,*** 10 November 1981.
7. *First Civil suit hearing in Bahasa,* ***New Straits Times,*** 2 December 1981.
8. *90pc of lower court cases in Bahasa,* ***New Sunday Times,*** 30 January 1983.
9. *The Suffian interview. Judges and jury trials,* by Tan Sri Dr. Tan Chee Khoon, ***Star,*** 12 November 1982.
10. *Bahasa in the courts: Too slow, says V-C,* ***New Straits Times,*** 28 May 1982.
11. *Where justice isn't blind to its own needs,* ***Star,*** 27 October 1981.
12. ***Star,*** 19 June 1981.
13. *Bahasa version of 60 laws await King's consent,* ***New Sunday Times,*** 3 October 1982, Kuala Lumpur.
14. (Headline mutilated), ***Star,*** February 1981. "According to the report, among the grounds given by the relevant authorities in defence of the claim that Bahasa Malaysia is incapable of being used as the medium in courts are: that laws continue to be written in English, there are no lawyers and judges who are proficient in Bahasa and that justice is more important than language. The report urges the authorities concerned to draft all future Bills for tabling in Parliament and State Assemblies directly in Bahasa Malaysia. The present practice is to draft the Bills in English and then translate them into Bahasa Malaysia. The problem arising from this, the report says, is that some sentences, phrases and words in Bahasa become discordanct because the translation follows closely the original copies which are in English."

    Also, *Bahasa still on trial,* ***Sunday Mail,*** 18 October 1981, Kuala Lumpur.

"As a lawyer says 'citing a principle of law and substantiating it with precedents requires a highly technical language like English.' Unless the corpus of legal works, the argument runs, is first translated into Bahasa, it would be difficult to use the national language in courts. . . . The negative attitude towards Bahasa is best evident in how lawyers view the Bahasa versions of the laws now being passed by Parliament."

"Statutes are now published in both Bahasa and English but almost everyone relies on the English version. What is worse, often the Bills themselves carry the statement that the English version is 'definitive.' It is obvious why the Bahasa version gathers dust, just like the Dewan's translations of terminology."

15. *Translate court judgements*, ***Star,*** 26 January 1983.
16. W. Twining, "The Concept of a National Legal Literature," in ***Legal Literature in Small Jurisdictions,*** W. Twining and J. Uglow, eds. (London: The Commonwealth Secretariat, 1981), pp. 7-21, esp. pp. 8-9.
17. *Lawyers: we have to use English,* ***Star,*** 17 January 1981, Penang, Fri. " 'Sheer nonsense and absolute rubbish'—that was how lawyers here viewed the suggestion of the Penang Bar Committee newsletter calling for the abolition of English law in the country. Lawyer R. Manecksha said the present legal system was already 'Malaysian-based.' There was no doubt that Bahasa Malaysia would be implemented in Malaysian courts one day. But Bahasa could only be implemented when lawyers and judicial officers could master the language."

    See also, *Bahasa still on trial,* ***Sunday Mail,*** 18 October 1981. "The opposition then, as it is now, however, was qualified. Lawyers then maintained that they were not against the ultimate use of Bahasa in principle. The bone of their contention was that trials in Bahasa were not feasible yet."
18. *Medical terms should not be a deterrent,* ***Malay Mail,*** 22 December 1980.
19. *Ministry tricked us, say sacked nurses,* ***Sunday Star,*** 25 January 1981.

    See also, *Minister to take up grouses of contract nurses,* ***New Straits Times,*** 2 February 1981.
20. *New thrusts in legal education,* ***New Straits Times,*** 18 March 1982.
21. ***Star,*** 20 December 1980. MTUC office bearers are listed as follows: President, P. P. Narayanan. Deputy President, Zainal Rampak. Vice Presidents, Mohamed bin Abas, A. J. Patrick, A. H. Ponniah, Sunny Wong, Mohamed Noh bin Katim, G. Perumal. Secretary-General,V. David. Deputy Secretary-General, G. Rajasekaran. Financial Secretary, V. Baradan. Deputy Financial Secretary; Mohamed bin Haji Yusof. Of these twelve names, four are Malay, one Chinese, and seven Indian.
22. Koid Swee Lian, "Legal Education in Malaysia: A Critical Analysis" (LLB dissertation, Universiti Malaya, 1981), p. 123.
23. Ahmad Ibrahim, *Legal Education in Malaysia,* in ***The Report of the First Malaysian Law Conference,*** (Kuala Lumpur, July 15-17, 1971), p. 117.
24. *Syariah: Poor response from Muslim lawyers,* ***New Straits Times,*** 1 December 1981, Ipoh, Mon. "No Muslim lawyer has come forward to appear in Syriah

courts in Perak since a new rule enabling them to do so was approved recently. The poor response might be because taking up Syariah court cases was not as lucrative as representing clients in the civil courts. They seem to think that Syarian court cases may be worth only $100 each."

"The spokesman also said for a $30 fee the lawyers could apply for a license to appear in Syariah courts from the president of the Perak Religious and Malay Customs Council. The applicants must be Muslims residing in Malaysia, who are conversant with Islam and Islamic laws. They must also be qualified to teach the religion in any states in Malaysia or have obtained a degree or diploma from an Islamic or any other university or a college, are proficient in *jawi*, romanised Malay and have a basic knowledge of Syariah court procedures."

25. *Dean: USM to introduce law studies from 1984,* ***New Straits Times,*** 24 November 1982.
26. *Special course for law students,* ***New Straits Times,*** 10 April 1982.
27. *Concessions for law students?,* ***New Straits Times,*** 6 July 1982.
28. Koid Swee Lian, "Legal Education in Mayalsia: A Critical Analysis"" (LLB dissertation, Universiti Malaya, 1981), p. 40.
29. *Lawyers: We have to use English,* ***Star,*** 17 January 1981.
30. *Suffian: courts cannot ban criminal drivers,* ***Star,*** 25 December 1980.
31. *Most clients don't know the charges,* ***New Straits Times,*** 5 April 1981.
32. Ibid., ***New Straits Times,*** 5 April 1981.
33. Ibid.
34. *Lawyer busy, so robbery case put off for 11th time,* ***Star,*** 13 August 1982.
35. *Gov't. move to beat the legal backlog,* ***Sunday Mail,*** 2 November 1980. "Deputy Minister in the Prime Minister's department Datuk Abdullah Abdul Rahman said the only way to solve this problem was by increasing the number of students doing law studies so that they could fill the vacancies."
36. *The Suffian interview, part 3. Judges and juries,* by Tan Sri Dr. Tan Chee Khoon, ***Star,*** 12 November 1982.
37. *Clock-in at lower courts—eight months later,* ***Star,*** 7 September 1982.
38. *90pc of lower court cases in Bahasa,* ***New Sunday Times,*** 30 January 1983.
39. *Most clients don't know the charges,* by Paulynn Chin and Calvin Goh, ***New Straits Times,*** 5 April 1981. "Lawyer R. Ponnudurias . . . Eighty per cent of our clients do not know what the charges against them are. They don't know the Sessions Court from the magistrates courts. . . . Some accused persons have no funds to engage a lawyer. They sometimes mislead the court. If they do not pay us we don't turn up. That's our prerogative."
40. *The Suffian interview, part 2. Need for a Law Reform Commission* by Tan Sri Dr. Tan Chee Khoon, ***Star,*** 11 November 1982.
41. *Bar "yes" to Law Reform Commission,* ***Star,*** 12 November 1982.
42. *Changes to Penal Code to protect religious freedom,* ***New Straits Times,*** 11 October 1982.

43. *Bar Council's move to help poor,* **New Straits Times,** 17 July 1982. "The LAC (Legal Aid Centre) will be based only in Kuala Lumpur, but if it proves functional, centres will be set up in other state. . . . 68 lawyers, of whom 22 are from outstation, have volunteered their services for this pilot project."

    See also, *Bar Council to give free legal aid,* **Star,** 17 July 1982.
44. *Malaysia to conduct own Bar exams,* **New Sunday Times,** 27 March 1983. "Right now, it costs the Government $24,000 per year to sponsor a law student in Britain. However, since students will not be studying the preparatory course for the Bar examinations locally, it will only cost $6,000 per student."
45. *Appeals to Privy Council may be stopped,* **New Straits Times,** 16 October 1981.
46. Editorial: *Anachronism,* **New Straits Times,** 27 October 1981.
47. *No plans yet to stop cases for Privy Council,* **New Straits Times,** 13 January 1982.
48. *Privy Council appeal to go,* **New Straits Times,** 26 October 1982.
49. **Star,** 5 March 1983, Kuala Lumpur, Fri. "The Government has agreed in principle to set up a Supreme Court, former Lord President Tun Mohamed Suffian said."
50. *Gov't. urged form Bahasa task force,* **New Straits Times,** 13 October 1982. "To further promote truly Malaysian values, Encik Shamsuri also suggested the use of the national dress at all official functions, including investiture ceremonies. He also suggested that the blowing of candles and cutting of birthday cakes at functions organised by the Government be replaced by reciting of prayers."

    See also, *Wear the songkok, judges told,* **Star,** 20 October 1982.
51. *"Use Bahasa in courts" call by Senators,* **New Straits Times,** 14 January 1982.
52. *Views on morals law "misconstrued,"* **Star,** 22 December 1982.
53. (headline mutilated), **Star,** 16 July 1982.

Chapter 4

1. *Taken to task for anti-Bahasa stand,* **New Straits Times,** 16 March 1983.

    See also, *Wanted—More time to master Bahasa,* **Star,** 16 March 1983.
2. *Why I spoke in English at Gerakan meeting: PM,* **New Straits Times,** 5 November 1980.
3. *I spoke in Mandarin after my speech: Dr. Goh,* **Star,** 15 October 1981.
4. *Pronouncing Bahasa Malaysia properly,* **New Straits Times,** 25 November 1982.
5. *Set up panels to help in Bahasa usage,* **New Straits Times,** 13 March 1981.

    See also, *Councillors told: Use Bahasa at meetings,* **Star,** 12 November 1981.

    See also, *Speak Bahasa, Councillors told,* **New Straits Times,** 12 November 1981.

6. *Bahasa: Don raps "Too many cooks,"* **Sunday Star,** 21 December 1980.
7. *Docs protest against Bahasa ruling,* **Star,** 17 May 1982.
8, *Teacher impeached for material contradictions,* **New Straits Times,** 14 December 1982.
9. *The Bahasa that is used in courts . . .,* **Star,** 8 October 1981. "On most occasions, it is the interpreter who comes to the rescue. Yesterday, a lawyer did not realise that his case was being mentioned in court although he was present. He only knew about it when he was told by the interpreter. The lawyer said later, 'The charge was read out in Bahasa Malaysia. I could not detect anything which resembled my case. I didn't know until I was told by the interpreter.' "
10. *"Your Honour" is out, "Tuan Mejistret" in,* **New Straits Times,** 9 October 1981.

    See also, *Rush to find the words,* **Star,** 17 October 1981.
11. *Medical exam blues,* **Malay Mail,** 15 March 1982.
12. *Bahasa: Don raps "Too many cooks,"* **Sunday Star,** 21 December 1980.
13. *Bahasa Cheer in Court,* by Sahaini Aznam, **Star,** 17 October 1981.

    See also, *The "Bahasa" that is used in court,* **Star,** 8 October 1981, Kuala Lumpur, Wed. "Bahasa Malaysia as it is used in courts can be quite amusing, even embarrassing. Sessions Court presidents and magistrates began hearing cases in Bahasa from Monday in compliance with a circular from the Chief Registrar. However, they allow 'bending' of the language rules and many of the sentences are a combination of Bahasa and English. The more amusing ones are the literal translations from English to Bahasa Malaysia."

    "Saya taruh sama engkau, engkau terbaring." ("I put it to you, you are lying.")

    "Saya akan apply for cost." ("I will apply for costs.")

    "Tidak halangan" ("No objections.")

    ". . . ditudah bawah Hak Cipta Act 1969," (". . . charge under the Copyrights Act 1969.")

    The proper way to address the magistrate and Sessions Court presidents also poses an intriguing question to the lawyers. Terms ranging from a simple "Tuan/Puan" to "Yang Berhormat" were used. But in Seremban, lawyers and DPPs are using "Yano Arif" as a substitute for "Your Honor."
14. *Unit to be set up to prevent Bahasa Malaysia pollution,* **New Straits Times,** 16 October 1980.

    See also, *Special unit to ensure correct usage of Bahasa,* **Star,** 17 December 1980.

    See also, *Bahasa: dewan steps up campaign on correct usage,* **Star,** 1 July 1981.
15. **Star,** 8 October 1981.
16. *"Refusal to learn the main obstacle,"* **New Straits Times,** 18 May 1982.
17. *Bahasa exams for lawyers in 1984,* **Star,** 25 June 1981.

    See also, *Bahasa test a "must" for lawyers soon,* **Star,** 21 October 1981.

See also, Editorial: *Constitution "barrier" has to go to rid lawyers of Bahasa prejudice,* ***Sunday Mail,*** 25 October 1981. "Would the requirement announced in Parliament last week that by 1984 all lawyers must have a Bahasa qualification for registration to practise then change the present situation? The Bar Councils reaction, according to reports, expressing surprise that the ruling calls for all lawyers, not just the new entrants to the profession, to possess Bahasa qualifications not only illustrates that prejudice dies hard but also raises doubts whether laws can change attitudes. Even if all lawyers accept the ruling and work for the paper qualifications there remains the question whether it would lead to the efficient and wide-spread use of Bahasa. For one, paper qualifications do not necessarily mean that these lawyers would switch to Bahasa."

18. *Pat on back for Johore Bar's Bahasa class,* ***Star,*** 11 November 1981.
19. *250 lawyers at Bahasa course,* ***New Straits Times,*** 18 June 1982. "The first part of the course dealt with the language and grammar while the second part concentrated on legal terminology."
20. *Bahasa cheer in court,* ***Star,*** 27 October 1981.

Chapter 5

1. *KL's infatuation with Japan waning?,* ***Nation,*** 14 March 1984, Bangkok. "In 1983, Malaysia's trade deficit with Japan was 1.7 billion ringgits (740 million US dollars). Lim See Yang, deputy governor of the Bank of Negara (central bank), warned that at the MAJECA (Malaysia-Japan Economic Association) meeting that the figure could more than double to 3.6 billion ringgits (1.57 billion US dollars) in 1985. But some Western diplomats here feel the current criticisms will not lead to cancellation of the *Look East* policy because the government is too committed to it."
2. *Hussein on national unity,* ***Sunday Mail,*** 2 November 1980.
3. *30pc target: Work harder, Malays told,* ***New Sunday Times,*** 30 November 1980.
4. (Headline mutilated), ***Star,*** 11 December 1980.
5. *Musa: Bahasa is now everybody's language,* ***Star,*** 25 February 1981.
6. *Bahasa good enough to go international,* ***New Straits Times,*** 22 November 1980.
7. *Proposal to use Bahasa at Asean conferences,* ***Sunday Star,*** 7 February 1982.

   See also, *Bahasa may become a world language yet,* ***Star,*** 21 October 1981.
8. *Rahim: Get Malay accepted for use in the UN,* ***Star,*** 21 December 1982.
9. *The dilemma of unifying a multilingual society,* by James Clad, ***Far Eastern Economic Review,*** 17 November 1983.
10. *How linguists can help promote use of Bahasa,* ***New Straits Times,*** 6 September 1982.
11. *Dewan's help in the proper use of Bahasa,* ***Sunday Mail,*** 11 July 1982.

12. *So brilliant, but oh so poor in Bahasa*, **Star,** 2 April 1981.

    See also, *Why the top city schools did badly in HSC exam*, **Star,** 20 March 1981.

13. *Why it is almost impossible for Malaysians to come to grips with our communal problems* by Suhaini Aznam, **Star,** 19 January 1983. "Malaysians as a whole are uncomfortable about discussing their fears about their own—or anyone else's race—openly. They are averse to hurting other people's feelings. Thus the true feelings of any community are only aired when its members meet out of earshot of other communities; or when like-minded academics get together."

14. For a breakdown of the election results, see *Mahathir turns the tide*, ***Far Eastern Economic Review,*** 30 April 1982.

15. *The press in a climate of fear*, by Mohideen Abdul Kader, ***Far Eastern Economic Review,*** 17 November 1983.

16. *What price loyalty?*, by Tan Sri Dr. Tan Chee Khoon, **Star,** 17 November 1982.

17. For a highly critical discussion of press restrictions, see *The press in a climate of fear* by Mohideen Abdul Kader, ***Far Eastern Economic Review,*** 17 November 1983.

18. *Use of Bahasa in the mass media*, **New Straits Times,** 16 October 1981.

    See also, *RTM criticised for not keeping to Bahasa*, **New Straits Times,** 28 August 1982. *Gov't.'s view in all tube shows going Bahasa*, **New Straits Times,** 26 November 1982. "The Government is examining the possibility of using Bahasa Malaysia in all television programmes. Information Minister Encik Mohamed Adib Adam said this was being done in stages as the Government had to consider the role of English as a second language."

    See also, *TV Malaysia to promote local culture*, **New Sunday Times,** 28 November 1982. *RTM's Bahasa—only plan*, **Star,** 4 December 1982. *RTM move to ensure proper use of Bahasa*, **New Straits Times,** 18 April 1983.

19. *Video boom: Gov't. to act*, **Star,** 21 August 1982, Penang, Fri. "The Government may take steps to impose some form of control over the video industry, Information Minister Encik Adib Adam said today. Encik Adib said the Ministry was concerned that loss of TV Malayia audience to video might hamper government efforts to disseminate national aspirations and values and channel information to the people."

Bibliography

Books and Monographs

Abdullah Taib and Mohamed Yusoff Ismail. 'The Social Structure.' In *The Political Economy of Malaysia* edited by E. K. Fisk and H. Osman-Rani. Kuala Lumpur: Oxford University Press, 1982, pp. 104-24.

Ahmad, I. 'Legal Education in Malaysia. ' In *The Report of the first Malaysian Law Conference*. Kuala Lumpur, July 15-17, 1971.

Ahmad, I. 'Parallel Systems of Law in Malaysia and Singapore,' *Jernal Undang - Undang,* June 1976, pp. 1-34.

Ampalavanar, R. *The Indian Minority and Political Change in Malaya 1945-1957*. Singapore: Oxford University Press, 1981.

Andaya, B. W. and Andaya, L. Y. *A History of Malaysia*. London: Macmillan, 1982.

Asmah, H. O. *Language Planning for Unity and Efficiency.* Kuala Lumpur: Penerbit Universiti Malaya, 1979.

Athuluthmudal, L. W. 'The Language of the Courts.' *Malaya Law Review,* Vol. 4, Singapore: University of Singapore, 1962, pp. 221-32.

Bartholomew, G. W. 'The Singapore Legal System.' In *Singapore: Society in Transition,* edited by Riaz Hassan. Kuala Lumpur: Oxford University Press, 1976.

Bates, E. *Language and Context: The Acquisition of Pragmatics.* New York: Academic Press, 1976.

Becker, H. S. and Geer, B. 'Latent Culture: A Note on the Theory of Latent Social Roles.' *Administrative Science Quarterly,* 1960, pp. 304-13.

Bell, R. T. *Sociolinguistics.* London: Batsford, 1976.

Bergman, P. *Trial Advocacy in a Nutshell*. St. Paul, Minn.: West Publishing Co., 1979.

Bhatia, V. *An Applied Discourse Analysis of English Legislative Writing*. Language Studies Unit Research Project, Birmingham Language Studies Unit, University of Aston in Birmingham, 1983.

Bromage, M. C. *DeValera and the March of a Nation*. New York: Noonday Press, 1956.

Brown, L. N. 'The Linguistic Regime of the European Communities: Some Problems of Law and Language.' Symposium: International Perspectives of Jurisprudence, *Valparaiso University Law Review,* Vol. 15, No. 2, 1981, pp. 319-41.

Brown, R. and Gilman, A. 'The Pronouns of Power and Solidarity.' In *Style in Language* by T. A. Sebeok. MIT Press, 1960, pp. 253-76.

Carlen, P. *Magistrates' Justice.* London: Martin Robertson, 1976.

Carlson, S. *Malaysia: Search for National Unity and Economic Growth.* Washington Papers, Vol. 3. Beverly Hills/London: Sage Publications, 1975.

Cham, B. N. 'Class and Communal Conflict in Malaysia.' *Journal of Contemporary Asia,* Vol. 5, No. 4, 1975, pp. 446-61.

Chandra, M. *Protector?* Penang: Aliran, 1979.

Chandra, M. 'Has the Communal Situation in Malaysia Worsened over the Last Decade? Some Preliminary Thoughts.' Modernization and National-Cultural Identity Seminar, Kuala Lumpur: Universiti Malaya, January 1983.

Chandriah A. R.; Ross-Larson, B; Noordin S; Tjoa H. G. *Issues in Contemporary Malaysia.* Kuala Lumpur: Heinemann, 1977.

Charrow, R. P. and Crandall, V. R. 'Lawyers' views of the Comprehensibility of Legal Language.' Presented at the fifth Annual Colloquim on New Ways of Analyzing Variation in English. Washington, D.C.: Georgetown University, October 1976.

Coulthard, R. M. *An Introduction to Discourse Analysis.* London: Longman, 1977.

Crystal, D. and Davy, D. *Investigating English Style.* London: Longman, 1969.

Danet, B. 'Language in the Legal Process.' *Law and Society,* Vol. 14:3. Denver, Colorado, 1980, pp. 445-564.

Danet, B; Hoffman, K. B.; Kermish, N. C.; Rafu, H. J.; and Stayman, D. G. 'An Ethnography of Questioning.' In *Language Use and the Uses of Language: Papers from the fifth Annual Colloquim on New Ways of Analyzing Variation,* edited by R. Shuy and A. Shnukal. Washington, D.C.: Georgetown Univ ersity Press, 1980.

Danet, B. and Kermish, N. C. 'Courtroom Questioning: A Sociolinguistic Perspective.' In *Psychology and Persuasion in Advocacy,* edited by L. N. Massery. Washington, D.C. Association of Trial Lawyers of America, National College of Advocacy, 1978.

Dworkin, R. M. 'Editorial.' In *The Philosophy of Law,* edited by R. M. Dworkin. Oxford: Oxford University Press, 1977, pp. 1-16.

Edmonds, J. 'Religion. Intermarriage and Assimilation: The Chinese in Malaysia.' *Race* X, 1968.

Ehlermann, C. D. 'The Interpretation of Community Law by the European Court.' In *The Interpretation of Community Law and the Role of the European Court.* London: UK Association of European Law, 1976.

Enloe, C. H. "Multi-Ethnic Politics: The Case of Malaysia." Ph.D. dissertation, Berkeley: University of California, 1967.

Enloe, C. H. 'Issues and Integration in Malaysia.' *Pacific Affairs, 1968, pp. 272-85.*

Esman, M. J. *Administration and Development in Malaysia.* Ithaca and London: Cornell University Press, 1972.

Federation of Malaya Legislative Council Debates. *Official Report*. Kuala Lumpur: Government Press, 1957.

Fishman, J. A. *Language and Nationalism: Two Integrative Essays*. Rowley, Mass.: Newbury House, 1972.

Fisk, E. K. 'Development in Malaysia.' In *The Political Economy of Malaysia*, edited by E. K. Fisk and H. Osman-Rani. Kuala Lumpur: Oxford University Press, 1982, p. 88-103.

Fisk, E. K. and Osman-Rani, H., eds. *The Political Economy of Malaysia*. Kuala Lumpur: Oxford University Press, 1982.

Funston, N. J. *Malay Politics in Malaysia*. Kuala Lumpur: Heinemann, 1980.

Gardner, S. W. "Ethnicity and Work: Occupational Distribution in an Urban Multi-Ethnic Setting in Georgetown, Panang, Malaysia." Ph.D. dissertation, Berkeley: University of California, 1975.

Goh, C. T. 'The Chinese in Malaysia: A Society in Transition.' Modernization and National-Cultural Identity Seminar, Kuala Lumpur: Universiti Malaya, January 1983.

Gullick, J. *Malaysia: Economic Expansion and National Unity*. London: Ernest Benn, 1981.

Gulliver, P. H. 'On Mediators.' *Social Anthropology and Law: ASA Monograph 14*, edited by I. Hamnett. London: Academic Press, 1977, pp. 15-52.

Gurdial, S. N. "The Position of the Unrepresented Accused in the Subordinated Courts in Malaysia." LLM thesis, Kuala Lumpur: Universiti Malaya, 1978.

Gurdial S. N. 'The Lawyer and the Public Interest.' Federation of Malaysia Consumers' Associations Seminar on Law and the Malaysian Consumer, Kuala Lumpur: Universiti Malaya, 13 May 1981.

Gurdial, S. N. 'Administration of Laws: A Study of the Access of the Common Man to the Law, its Process and Institutions.' Consumers Association of Penang 1982 Seminar, Penang, 19-23 November 1982.

Harris, S. 'Questions as a Mode of Control in Magistrates'Courts.' *International Journal of the Society of Language*, 1982.

Hart, H. L. A. *The Concept of Law. Oxford*. Clarendon Press, 1961.

Heng, P. K. 'The Social and Ideological Origins of the Malaysian Chinese Association.' The Eighth Conference of the International Association of Historians of Asia, Kuala Lumpur, 25-29 August 1980.

Higgins. B. 'Development Planning.' In *The Political Economy of Malaysia*, edited by E. K. Fisk and H. Osman-Hani. Kuala Lumpur: Oxford University Press, 1982, pp. 148-83.

Hooker, M. B. *Adat Laws in Modern Malaysia*. Kuala Lumpur: Oxford University Press, 1972.

Hooker, M. B. *A Concise Legal History of South-East Asia*. Oxford: Clarendon Press, 1978.

Hua, W. Y. *Class and Communalism in Malaysia*. London: Zed Books, 1983.

Husin, A. S. *The Malays*. Kuala Lumpur: Heinemann, 1981.

Husin, A. S. 'Social Relations in Malaysia: Ethnic and Class Factors,' Modernization and National-Cultural Identity Seminar, Kuala Lumpur: Universiti Malaya, January 1983.

Inglis, C. 'Educational Policy and Occupational Structures in Pan-Malaysia.' In *Issues in Malaysian Development,* edited by J. C. Jackson and M. Rudner. Kuala Lumpur: Heinemann, 1979, pp. 205-32.

Joos, M. *The Five Clocks: A Linguistic Excursion into the Five Styles of English Usage.* New York: Harcourt, Brace and World, 1961.

Koh Tong Ngee, P. 'The Legal Profession: A Preliminary Hearing on Complaints, Discipline, and Professional Standards.' Consumers' Association of Penang 1982 Seminar, Penang, 19-23 November 1982.

Koid, S. L. "Legal Education in Malaysia: A Critical Analysis." LLB dissertation, Kuala Lumpur: Universiti Malaya, 1981.

Kullada, K. " 'Official Nationalism" under King Chulalongkorn.' Thai Studies Conference, Bangkok: King Chulalongkorn University, August 1984.

Laffin, J. *The Arab Mind.* London: Cassell, 1975.

Lang, R. 'Interpreters in Local Courts in Papua New Guinea.' In *Language and Politics,* edited by W. M. O'Barr and S. F. O'Barr. The Hague: Mouton, 1976, pp. 327-66.

Lee, K. H. 'Malaya: New State and Old Elites.' In *Asia—The Winning of Independence,* edited by by R. Jeffrey. London: Macmillan, 1981, pp. 213-57.

Lev, D. S. 'Judicial Authority and the Struggle for an Indonesian Rechtsstaat.' *Law and Society Review.* Vol. 13, No. 1, 1979, pp. 37-71.

Lim, H. S. "Unrepresented Accused Persons in Lower Courts." LLB dissertation, Kuala Lumpur: Universiti Malaya, 1975.

Lind, E. A. and O'Barr, W. M. 'The Social Significance of Speech in the Courtroom.' In *Language and Social Psychology,* edited by N. Giles and R. St. Clair. Oxford: Blackwell, 1979, pp. 66-87.

Mahathir, b. Mohamed. *The Malay Dilemma.* Kuala Lumpur: Federal Publications, 1970, 1982.

Malinowski, B. 'Introduction.' In *Law and Order in Polynesia,* by H. Hogbin. New York: Harcourt and Brace, 1934.

Mandelbaum, D. G., ed., *Edward Sapir: Culture, Language and Personality—Selected Essays.* Berkeley: University of California, 1966.

Mauzy, D. K. *Barison Nasional.* Kuala Lumpur and Singapore: Marican and Sons, 1983.

McVey, R. 'Culture, Separatism, and the Paradoxes of the Nation-State.' MS., 1983, p. 18.

Means, G. P. *Malaysian Politics.* London: Hodder and Stoughton, 1970, 1976.

Mead, R. "An Analysis of Small-Group Discourse and its Application." Ph.D. dissertation, Birmingham University, 1980.

Mead, R. Review article: "Asmah Haji Omar 1979." *English Language Research Journal,* No. 4, Birmingham University, 1983.

Mead, R. *Courtroom Discourse.* English Language Research Monograph No. 9, Birmingham University, 1985.

Milne,, R. S. and Mauzy, D. *Politics and Government in Malaysia.* Singapore: Times Books International/ISEAS, 1970, revised 1980.

Mohamed, Aris H. O. 'Malay Ethnic Identity in Historical Perspective.' The Eighth Conference of the International Association of Historians of Asia, Kuala Lumpur, 25-29 August 1980.

Mohamed Idris, S. M. 'Opening Address.' Consumers' Association of Penang 1982 Seminar, Penang, 19-23 November 1982.

Morawetz, T. *The Philosophy of Law.* New York: Macmillan, 1980.

Platt, J. and Weber, H. *English in Singapore and Malaysia.* Kuala Lumpur: Oxford University Press, 1980.

Ratnam, J. J. *Communalism and the Political Process in Malaya.* Kuala Lumpur: University of Malaya Press, 1965.

Riaz Hassan, ed. *Singapore: Society in Transition.* Kuala Lumpur: Oxford University Press, 1976, pp. 155-88.

Roff, M. 'The Politics of Language in Malay.' *Asian Survey* Vol. 7, No. 5, May 1967, pp. 316-28.

Roff, W. R. *The Origins of Malay Nationalism.* Second Edition. Kuala Lumpur: University of Malaya Press, 1974.

Shuy, R. W. and Larkin, D. K. 'Linguistic Considerations in the Simplication/ Classification of Insurance Policy Language.' Washington, D.C.: Georgetown University and the Center for Applied Linguistics, 1978.

Sinclair, J. M. 'Discourse in Relation to Language Structure and Semiotics.' Paper prepared in advance for participants in Burg Wartenstein Symposium No. 66. New York: Wenner-Gren Foundation for Anthropological Research, August 8-17, 1975.

Sinclair, J. M. and Coulthard, R. M. *Towards an Analysis of Discourse.* London: Oxford University Press, 1975.

Steiner, G. 'The Language Animal.' In *Extra-Territorial: Papers on Literature and the Language Revolution.* New York: Atheneum, 1968.

Stubbs, M. *Discourse Analysis.* Oxford: Blackwell, 1983

Swales, J. 'The Case of Cases in English for Academic Legal Purposes.' *IRAL,* 20 February 1982.

Swales, J. and Bhatia, V. K. 'An Approach to Linguistic Study of Legal Documents. A paper given at the SSRC 'Law and Language'Seminar, Oxford, 24-25 September 1980.

Tongue, R. K. *The English of Singapore and Malaysia.* Singapore: Eastern Universities Press, 1979.

Twining, W. 'The Concept of a National Legal Literature.' In *Legal Literature in Small Jurisdictions,* edited by W. Twining and J. Uglow. London: The Commonwealth Secretariat, 1981, pp. 7-21.

Twining, W. and Uglow, J. 'Introduction.' *Legal Literature in Small Jurisdictions.* London: The Commonwealth Secretariat, 1981, pp. 1-6.

Vikor, L. 'Language Policy and Language Planning in Indonesia and Malaysia.' In *Indonesia and Malaysia,* edited by T. Svensson and P. Sorenson. London and Malmo: Curzon Press, 1983, pp. 47-74.

Von Vorys, K. *Democracy without Consensus.* Kuala Lumpur: Oxford University Press, 1976.

Wang, G. *Community and Nation.* Singapore: Heinemann, 1981.

Wee, V. 'Buddhism in Singapore.' In *Singapore: Society in Transition,* edited by Riaz Hassan. Kuala Lumpur: Oxford University Press, 1976, pp. 155-88.

Whorf, B. L. *Language, Thought and Reality.* Cambridge, Mass.: MIT, 1962.

Winch, P. *The Idea of a Social Science and Its Relation to Philosophy.* London: Routledge and Kegan Paul, 1958.

Wilson, A. B. 'Education, Mobility and Expectations of Youth in Malaysia.' In *Cultural Pluralism in Malaysia: Polity, Military, Education, Religion, and Social Class,* edited by J. A. Lent. Special Report No. 14, Center for Southeast Asian Studies, Northern Illinois University, 1977, pp. 58-70.

Winstedt, R. *The Malays: A Cultural History.* 1947. Revised by Than Seong Chee. Singapore: Graham Brash, 1981.

Wong, I. 'Malaysian English as a New Variety of English: The Structural Aspect.' Paper given at the sixteenth Regional Seminar, SEAMEO Regional Language Centre, Singapore, 1981.

Wu, M. A. *An Introduction to the Malaysian Legal System.* Kuala Lumpur: Heinemann, 1975.

Zakaria, H. A. 'The Political Structure.' In *The Political Economy of Malaysia,* edited by E. K. Fisk and H. Osman-Rani. Kuala Lumpur: Oxford University Press, 1982, pp. 88-103.

Zainudin, S. M. and Zulkifly, O. 'The Economic Structure.' In *The Political Economy of Malaysia,* edited by E. K. Fisk and H. Osman-Rani. 1982, pp. 125-47.

Newspapers and Periodicals

Malay Mail (Kuala Lumpur), various months 1980, 1981, 1982.

Nation (Bangkok), 14 March 1984.

New Straits Times (Kuala Lumpur), various months 1980, 1981, 1982, 1983.

New Sunday Times (Kuala Lumpur), various months 1980, 1981, 1982, 1983.

Star (Kuala Lumpur), various months 1980, 1981, 1982, 1983.

Sunday Mail (Kuala Lumpur), various months 1980, 1981, 1982.

Sunday Star, (Kuala Lumpur), various months 1980, 1981, 1982, 1983.

All England Law Reports (London), Vol. 230, 1954.

Asiaweek (Hong Kong), 17 December 1982.

Far Eastern Economic Review, (Hong Kong), 30 April 1982; 3 March 1983, 17 November 1983.

Insaf (Kuala Lumpur: Bar Council), January 1983.

The Magistrate (London), Vol. 31, No. 9, September 1981.

Practice Directions (London), 15 January 1954.

Suara Peguam. (Penang: Penang Bar Committee), October 1980.

Weekly Law Review (London), Vol. 1, 1960.

Index

O

P

Q

R

Z